PENGUIN BO

NATURE MADE RIDICU

Miles Kington was born in 1941 and began the research for this book shortly afterwards at the age of six, when he ate some grass and was very sick. One of the first nature books he was given was an observer's book of grasses and reeds, which contained about 500 drawings in black and white, all more or less the same, but which did not mention that eating grass made you sick. From this he deduced that nature books told you far too much, except about the really important things, and a subsequent life comparison between nature books and nature itself has given him no reason to change his mind. Hence this book.

At the moment he writes a daily humorous column for *The Times* called 'Moreover . . .', but his great ambition is to replace David Attenborough at the BBC and make a programme called *Life on Earth in Ten Minutes Flat*, as he thinks nature films are also far too detailed.

Miles Kington lives and works in Notting Hill, where he studies all the foxes, hawks, jays and other forms of wild life who now find it too dangerous or pesticidal to live in the country.

Penguin also publish the following books by Miles Kington: *Let's Parler Franglais!*, *Let's Parler Franglais Again!*, *Parlez-Vous Franglais?*, *Let's Parler Franglais One More Temps* and *Moreover . . .*, a selection from his column in *The Times*.

To Jackie,
happy 21st 13/2/85.

Paul

Miles Kington

NATURE MADE RIDICULOUSLY SIMPLE

or

HOW TO IDENTIFY ABSOLUTELY EVERYTHING

PENGUIN BOOKS

Penguin Books Ltd, Harmondsworth, Middlesex, England
Penguin Books, 40 West 23rd Street, New York, New York 10010, U.S.A.
Penguin Books Australia Ltd, Ringwood, Victoria, Australia
Penguin Books Canada Ltd, 2801 John Street, Markham, Ontario, Canada L3R 1B4
Penguin Books (N.Z.) Ltd, 182–190 Wairau Road, Auckland 10, New Zealand

First published by Hamish Hamilton Ltd 1983
Published in Penguin Books 1984

Copyright © Miles Kington, 1983
Illustrations copyright © Tim Jacques, 1983
All rights reserved

Made and printed in Great Britain by
Richard Clay (The Chaucer Press) Ltd,
Bungay, Suffolk

for Caroline

Contents

Introduction

This book has been written in an attempt to reverse a pernicious trend started in 1965 by the Duke of Edinburgh, when he lent his name to the publication of Keble Martin's *Concise British Flora.*

I am sorry to start like this. I realise it is more normal to establish the credentials of a nature book with a preface by a member of the Royal Family, rather than an attack on one, but it had to be done sooner or later. The plain fact of the matter is that Keble Martin's book, with its 1,480 coloured drawings of wild flowers, caught the public fancy and started a leisurely stampede of nature guides which became more and more detailed, more and more comprehensive. But they also, and this is the vital point, made nature *harder and harder to identify.*

If, for instance, you find a yellow flower which looks like a cross between a dandelion and a coltsfoot, you can turn to Keble Martin for help and browse through the pages devoted to what botanists call the *Compositae,* or what you and I would call yellow flowers which look like something between a dandelion and a coltsfoot. There you will find a picture of your yellow flower. In fact, you will find fifteen pictures, all virtually identical, and all called *Hieracium.*

While frowning over these yellow look-alikes, you will find your eye caught by Mr Keble Martin's recommendation that you buy Mr H W Pugsley's book on the *Hieracia.* 'Mr Pugsley has given us a clear picture of the genus with descriptions of 260 species. The following notes are only abbreviated extracts . . . together with short descriptions of 23 sample species.' In other words, there are not fifteen yellow flowers doing a Mike Yarwood on each other; there are two hundred and sixty trying to fool you.

Shaken, you come to the realisation that not only are you never going to identify your yellow flower, but that you have blundered into a world where the author is apologising for presenting only fifteen out of a possible 260 nearly identical flowers. It is my contention that Keble Martin should have expressed remorse for having presented as many as fifteen, and for not giving an English name to *any* of them. He should have abjectly apologised for calling his book Concise; all he meant by that was, concise compared to Mr Pugsley *who devoted one book to one flower*. To the rest of us there was nothing concise about his voluminous book of drawings, all of which slide imperceptibly from one to another. Nor is there anything concise about the flood of books which have followed Keble Martin, with or without endorsements by Prince Philip.

That botanists feel nagging guilt about this wholesale confusion of the public is shown by a quick reference to Collins's *The Wild Flowers of Britain and Northern Europe* which came out in 1974. Turn to the pages of yellow flowers and you find this: 'Hawkweeds, *Hieracium.* An exceptionally variable and difficult group, with some hundreds of microspecies. Here only four major groupings can be illustrated.'

Well, this is better. The authors have softened enough to give the plant an English name. They have reduced the number of look-alikes to four from fifteen. And they have even hinted at an apology for the whole thing being difficult. A move in the right direction. But a move so small and grudging that it can hardly comfort all those readers wandering through the British countryside, a book in their left hand, a flower in their right hand, and a look of unhappy, baffled terror on their faces.

What is needed to reverse the damage of nearly twenty years, started in an unholy alliance of Church and Crown by the Rev. Keble Martin and Prince Philip, is something drastic, something explosive and revolutionary. Which brings us to this book. *Nature Made Ridiculously Simple* is based on the following principles, which are revolutionary only because they depend on common sense, not science.

People like to identify things.

It is possible to identify anything.

Identification is made easier not by offering more choice of models, but *less* choice.

No part of nature should ever be divided into more than ten species.

There is a great thirst among the public for a book that will leave them feeling happy, not confused by profusion. People are unhappy today because they have too much freedom, in the words of Quentin Crisp. (Admittedly, he wasn't thinking of nature study. In fact, nature is not his thing. He once said to me: 'As an art class model, I have a prejudice against still life of any kind. You see, it poses for free.')

That is why *The Country Diary of an Edwardian Lady* was so wildly popular. In trying to explain its success people have generally been baffled. It couldn't have been the rather insipid verse she copied out, nor her banal observations of the local weather, nor even the attractive brown pages; suitable though they are for recycling into diaries, carrier bags, memo pads and so on, brown pages are not enough in themselves to create a best-seller.

No, what drew people to the book was that, quite by accident, it offered them a simplified guide to nature, a view of birds and flowers that they could respond to. The Edwardian Lady did not write: 'This morning I sketched a thrush, one of the 340 main kinds of thrush as described so well in Mr Pugsley's big book on thrushes.' She wrote: 'This morning I sketched a thrush.' It isn't great English, but by God you can identify with it. And you can identify a thrush from it.

The idea for this book was also born curiously enough in 1965, the year Prince Philip gave the royal assent. I was living in a small flat in London, with access to a garden. At the end of the garden there was a tall tree, with roundish leaves, which was not like any tree I knew. I bought a book full of trees. For much of the summer I compared my tree with the many trees in the book. None of them quite fitted, but the nearest to it seemed to be what they called a *Robinia Locusta*, or Pseudoacacia. 'It's a false acacia, actually.' I would tell friends.

Quite how false I found out in the autumn, when it proceeded to drop on the lawn a large number of walnuts.

Now, a botanist would sneer at me for confusing a walnut which has big leaves with a pseudoacacia, which does not. The point is that if the scale is not made clear, the leaves of both look the same sort of shape and have the same sort of arrangement. All I knew was that however good a tree book it was, there was something basically wrong with it.

I know now what was wrong with it. It offered me too much freedom, too much choice. At the very least it should have limited itself to a tree called 'a pseudoacacia, or walnut'.

This book, then, is for all those people who have ever been puzzled by a comprehensive guide to nature. It is for people who want to know, not the Latin name of an English thing, but what to call it so that other people will know what they're talking about. It is for people who, up to now, have not dared even talk about nature.

It is for people like David Barlow, in fact. Being fellow-members of Instant Sunshine, we do a lot of driving and talking together (he drives, I talk), and on one of our journeys I discovered he was incapable of identifying any tree whatsoever. To make a start, I pointed out an elder tree with its bunches of white flowers the size of Bath Olivers. He quickly learnt to identify it. We might have progressed further, except that he was so happy with the idea of knowing that flowering trees were elders, that to this day he believes there are two kinds of trees: elders, which flower, and non-elders, which do not.

Reducing all trees to two different species is a very advanced form of thinking, which I am not quite ready for and which, in addition, would not produce a very long book. So I would now like to restate my fourth principle.

No part of nature should ever be divided into more than ten species, but not less than ten either.

There are lots of nature guides that claim to be concise, but this one is different. It does not claim to be concise. It *is* concise.

Just how concise is shown by the fact that I intend this introduction to be the longest part of the book.

How to identify absolutely anything in Nature

A Step-by-Step Guide

How this key works: as soon as you have observed something in nature which you wish to identify and know more about, though not much more about, work your way through this little questionnaire. Unlike most keys, which are as stern as exam papers, this one is designed to be friendly and informal, so if you lose your way in the middle, don't worry. Either start again or, even better, discard the thing you're trying to identify and move on to something else.

1 Is it alive, or is it dead? If live, see 2. If dead, see 18. If it seems to be shamming, give it a prod.

LIVE

2 If it is alive, it is either stuck in the same place all its life (a plant — see 3) or can move about freely (not a plant — see 8).

Very occasionally you will come across things that can move about, but not very freely. This is almost certain to be a tethered goat, a wounded animal or something stuck in a cobweb. Whichever it is, obey the country code and leave well alone; they are private property, belonging respectively to a *Guardian* reader, the RSPCA and a spider. In any case, none of them is a true species in its own right.

LIVE, STATIONARY

3 Live things stuck in the same place for life, or plants. These are now classified according to their height. If they are under one inch, see 4. If between one inch and six feet, see 5. If between six feet and fifteen feet, see 6. If anywhere between fifteen feet and twenty thousand feet, see 7.

4 Live things stuck in the same place, under one inch. These are mosses, lichens, seaweeds, lawns, etc. SEE SECTION 1 — Moulds.

5 Live things stuck in the ground, up to six feet. If they are basically green, SEE SECTION TWO — Flowers. If they have no trace of green at all, SEE SECTION THREE — Fungi.

6 Live things stuck in the ground, six to fifteen feet. SEE
SECTION FOUR — Bushes.

Some flowers, by the way, manage to grow over six feet but can
easily be trimmed back to avoid confusion with bushes.

7 Live things, stuck in the ground, over fifteen feet. Unless you are
lucky enough to have come across a giraffe with its feet caught,
SEE SECTION FIVE — Trees.

LIVE, MOVING

8 Live things that can move around. But how is your object moving
around? It may be flying (see 9), walking (see 12), swimming (see
16) or floating upside down on water (see 17).

9 Live, flying things. These are subdivided strictly into things that
fly straight (see 10) and things that fly all over the place (see 11).

10 Things that fly straight. SEE SECTION SIX — Birds.

11 Things that refuse to fly straight. SEE SECTION SEVEN —
Insects With Wings.

12 Live, walking things. Some further observation is needed here
— how many legs does it have? If none, see 13; if two, it is either a
bird taking a rest (see 10) or a fellow country-lover (see chapter on
Your Fellow Country-Lovers); if four legs, see 14; if six, eight or
more, see 15.

Things with odd numbers of legs — three, five, seven, etc — do
exist but they are very rare. Count again.

13 Live, walking things, no legs. This is not walking in the normal
sense of the word, slithering really. SEE SECTION EIGHT —
Creepy Crawlies.

14 Live, walking things, four legs. SEE SECTION NINE —
Animals.

15 Live, walking things, six to a thousand legs. SEE SECTION
TEN — Insects With No Wings But Lots Of Legs.

16 Live, swimming things. These are usually but not invariably
fish. SEE SECTION ELEVEN — Things That Can Swim A Width.

17 Live things, floating upside down on the water. Actually, they
may also be the right way up, but as they are all perfectly
symmetrical in design it is very hard to tell and doesn't really
matter. Either way, SEE SECTION TWELVE — Hover-creatures.

DEAD

18 Dead things are never given much attention in nature guide books; I have seen some that did not mention a single dead thing. But there is a rich variety in dead nature, ranging from the mighty cloud to the humble pebble. The main clue to its identity lies in its habitat. So, observe whether your dead thing is part of the ground (see 19), lying on the ground (see 20), lying on the beach (see 21), stuck in the ground but not part of it (see 22), floating in the water (see 23), flying almost within reach (see 24) or flying way out of reach (25).

DEAD, STATIONARY

19 Dead, part of the ground. SEE SECTION THIRTEEN — Geology.
20 Dead, lying on the ground. SEE SECTION FOURTEEN — Nature's Refuse System.
21 Dead things lying on the beach. These are sometimes erroneously referred to as shore life. SEE SECTION FIFTEEN — Dead Things Lying On The Beach.
22 Dead things stuck in the ground. SEE SECTION SIXTEEN — Dutch Elm Disease.

DEAD, MOVING

23 Dead things floating in the water. SEE SECTION SEVENTEEN — Jetsam, Flotsam, Etcsam.
24 Dead things flying almost within reach. They look so easy to catch, but they never are, are they? SEE SECTION EIGHTEEN — Dead Things That Can Fly Faster Than You Can Run.
25 Dead things flying way out of reach. SEE SECTION NINETEEN — Basic Clouds.

And there you have all nature reduced to nineteen easy categories, though I feel it could be reduced further.

There are, in fact, three categories which I haven't mentioned, two of which cannot be illustrated or even observed. One is Things You Can Hear But Not See (such as crickets, woodpeckers, cuckoos) and the other is Things You Can Neither Hear Nor See (including moles, voles, trout and worms that leave spiral casts on the beach). I shall work these into the pre-existing nineteen categories.

The other category not so far mentioned is Young Of The Species. Nature guides, especially bird books, are spreading confusion these days by paying more and more attention to the fact that, when young, nature can look very different from its grown-up version. This seems to me all part of the unhealthy trend in human society to put too much spotlight on the young, their clothes and records, and it's worth calling a halt before someone issues a guide to punk nature.

So, if you do spot the young of a species, don't respond to its craving for attention. Come back later when it has grown up a bit.

Section One

Fuzz

Sensational journalists sometimes refer to something called the greenhouse effect, by which they mean that every time we use an aerosol, chemical deposits accumulate in the upper atmosphere which will raise the earth's temperature, melt the polar regions and eventually turn Guildford into a seaside resort.

But anyone who has spent any time in a greenhouse will know there are far more noticeable and important greenhouse effects. One is the mysterious accumulation of wooden boxes which fall to bits if you pick them up. Another is the tendency of small pots to get jammed together and to break when you separate them. The most common, though, is the tendency of the greenhouse floor to get covered in fuzzy stuff which seems neither quite dead nor alive.

This particular greenhouse effect is already present in nature, unlike the wooden box and jammed pot syndromes. The whole of the world is covered in greater or lesser degree by a sort of fuzz. If nature began life in a primordial soup, we have now got on to the primordial salad course.

This section, needless to say, divides that fuzz into ten different species.

LAWN

Lawn is the tidiest fuzz there is. It is sometimes said that lawns in gardens are totally unnatural. What nonsense! If anything in gardens is unnatural, it is deck chairs, swings swinging from trees, stone gnomes and, of course, greenhouses. Lawn, which is a natural mix of grass, clover, reeds and ant-hills, occurs wild on many a Chiltern hillside, all over Yorkshire, throughout Ireland and alongside most motorways. Indeed, lawn in the wild is often neater than garden lawn.

Lawn is fuzz *which has got its act together.*

MOULD

Rather carelessly, mould has got a bad name for itself. Most of the time it grows inoffensively on the parts of nature that other growths can't be bothered to grow on — white on land, green at the seaside — but occasionally it has made the tactical mistake of growing on things in the kitchen which we think are useful: tomatoes, mushrooms, bread and so on. Even then, it was partly our fault as we left the things lying around so long that mould thought we were finished with them.

If you think it is disgusting, remember that it is no more disgusting than snow. If you still think it's disgusting, I would keep clear of woods; most trees get mould.

LICHEN

Lichen is lawn which thinks it's moss, or perhaps moss which thinks it's lawn — either way, it's a dried-out version of both and always looks dead. It likes growing (or dying) on rocks, walls, churches, the side of the tree facing Iceland, and posters for holidays in Sweden. It has a range of five different colours: rust-red, rust-brown, rust-orange, rust-green and off-rust.

What marks lichen off from all other moulds is that nobody is quite sure how to pronounce it. Some say 'liken', some rhyme it with 'kitchen'. When you're writing a book about it, luckily, this is not a problem you have to worry about.

MOSS

Moss is simply lawn trying to grow in wet conditions. I once knew
a man who had a garden in such boggy country that when he built
a tennis court, he referred to the game played thereon as moss
tennis. It was quite fun, if you don't mind balls not bouncing.

EXPORT REJECT SEEDCAKE

Nature's reproductive system, at most levels, operates the same
way that informed opinion tells us the Chinese will fight World
War III: send out 500,000, and one should get through. In other
words, for every one seed that grows into a mighty tree, half a
million seeds bite the dust, except that they don't bite the dust —
they lie around in a kind of sludge under the tree, unable to
believe that they will never germinate. They get eaten, washed
away or rotted down.

This is most noticeable in London for a few days every summer, when all the plane seeds in the city blow around dangerously in bicyclists' faces and I, personally, put on a pair of motor bike goggles. The rest of the year I use these goggles for wearing when I am chopping onions — very effective against the tear-producing chemicals of that vegetable.

On one hot summer's day I went to answer the doorbell in the middle of an onion-slicing session and opened the door wearing only shorts and goggles, waving a sharp knife. The Jehovah's Witness outside fled at once.

A slight diversion, perhaps, but you don't often find nature guides telling you how to deal with unwanted missionaries.

SEAWEED

Any large green object which drapes itself artistically over the seaside rocks, along the high water mark or round your knees when you swim, can be classed as seaweed though I have always thought that sealawn would be a more marketable name.

What makes seaweed very special is that it is the only thing outside the fish and bird kingdoms that actually migrates. When you see seaweed aimlessly drifting around in the sea, it is in its own quiet way setting out on an immense summer cruise to warmer parts, the Mediterranean perhaps, or off to the Sargasso Sea to visit relations and swap gossip. Months later, through some miraculous homing device that we don't quite understand yet, it returns to the very same spot near Skegness or off the Mumbles. No wonder it flops across the rocks. It's knackered.

Its only natural enemies are children, who try to turn it into weather-forecasting devices, and the Welsh, who try to turn it into bread. Both attempts are disastrously unsuccessful.

There are two basic species of seaweed, if you're interested in further study; the kind you can pop in your fingers and the kind you can't.

LANDWEED, OR THREE DAY BEARD

Lying close to the ground, about 0.5 centimetres underneath, are vast quantities of lawn seeds, waiting only for a mixture of warm weather and wet to germinate. In the right conditions this produces a sort of green four o'clock shadow right across the land, almost visible on satellite photographs.

The nearest equivalent in human terms is the start of the London or New York marathon; thousands of little pathetic organisms struggling for a chance to make glory. Most of them won't last the course. Don't bother with either.

CUCKOOSPIT

It's odd how the cuckoo gets blamed for so much. Not only for throwing little birds out of nests and for causing letters to *The Times*, but for spitting. Those blobs of froth on grass are not cuckoospit at all, of course. For one thing, birds cannot spit; for another thing, those blobs are caused by farmers salivating into the undergrowth to signify the striking of a bargain.

PONDSPAWN

In spring, many ponds are surrounded by a kind of jelly with little black dots inside. Throw the first 499,999 away and keep the next. It will develop into one of the glories of nature, the tadpole, which is shaped as excitingly and beautifully as an Exocet or an avocado pear. Unfortunately, it then develops into one of the failures of nature, the frog, which goes on to seek out its natural enemy — the motor car — and be crushed by it.

CHURCH IVY

Any plant which climbs up another plant, or across a wall, or over an abandoned garden roller, or up your legs if tales about the fertility of rain forests are true, can be classified as ivy until you are more expert.

Ivy is usually classified as a parasite, or at least a hanger-on, which shows how little most naturalists follow things through. If an ivy plant completely covers a tree and the tree then dies, the ivy will continue growing in the shape of the tree *even when the tree rots and vanishes.* The same is true if the ivy gets to the top of the tree and continues without it.

The great dream, the so-far unrealised ambition, of the ivy world is to do the same to a church. What finer coup could there be than to have a church-shaped ivy plant *with no church inside?* There is already believed to be a castle in Ireland which is ²/₃ ivy.

It is dangerous to eat ivy. The same is true of churches.

Section Two

Flowers

This section is basically an attempt to start undoing the damage caused by naturalists who lump things together in families. These families are always based on highly dubious principles, usually on the idea that if two things look totally dissimilar, they probably belong to the same family. This is understandable in human society, where most people spend most of their time altering their appearance or moving vast distances in order to be dissociated from relatives, but in higher forms of life like flowers this is unlikely.

Naturalists tie themselves in all sorts of knots to explain their idea of families. Here is Gerald Durrell in *The Amateur Naturalist*: —

'Although conifers bear flowers of a sort, there are technical differences between conifer flowers and the flowers of a "flowering plant" which mean that conifers are not included in the group called Flowering Plants. Also, not all conifers are evergreens — larches are conifers that shed their leaves in autumn, and so they are deciduous conifers. And, strangely enough, not all conifers bear cones; the juniper is one that bears soft fleshy berries instead.'

Well, all I can say is that I am glad flowers cannot read, or they would be mightily confused. The way botanists divide up flowers reminds me of the way Africa was divided into countries by politicians.

Here are the main ten types of flower. If any flower thinks he does not fit into one of these, he can contact me chez Hamish

25

Hamilton, but mark your envelope carefully; they publish Mr Durrell's book as well.

GREATER HEDGE FROTH

Flowers January to December and grows mainly in hedges, though it can also be found in fields, woods, ditches, farmyards, car parks, railway stations and bomb sites. Reaching a height of between one and six feet, Greater Hedge Froth is instantly recognisable from its habit of growing in colonies of about three hundred or, more occasionally, quite alone.

The tiny white (or red or yellow or blue) flowers are grouped together at the top of the stalk, facing upwards towards the sun or botanist, and so arranged that, when the petals are counted in a circular direction, the one you started from has slightly changed position by the time you get back to it. Somewhat confusing from close up, this plant is probably better identified from a motor car or even a passing train.

Very common in Kent and Surrey, it is equally common elsewhere. The stems are almost invariably green.

STINKING SEA VEGETABLE

Britain's only exclusively seaside flower, the Stinking Sea Vegetable is found widely in such marine habitats as cliffs, beach huts, sand dunes, yacht trailer parks, golf courses, weed sanctuaries and gardens of cottages called Seaview. Its battle to survive against floods, tides, sand and little boys called Come Here Kevin leave it little time to spend on its personal appearance, and it has become tough, dark green, thick and quite unmemorable.

There is no particular odour attached to it, despite its name; it just looks as if it stinks. The name 'vegetable' arose because if it is boiled for about half an hour it doesn't taste much of anything, and was much used in the Middle Ages instead of spinach.

At one time Stinking Sea Vegetable was only found for a restricted period, but now that there is a plentiful supply of cheap imported foodstuff, it is available all the year round.

GOLDEN MEADOW THING

This welcome bloom, the harbinger of spring, is one of the first flowers to appear after the cold of winter and one of the last to go away. But, despite its lone arrival and its distinctive yellow, blue, purple, red, white or orange petals, it is not always easy to identify. The best way is to eliminate all other nine possibilities, as one tends to do when choosing a dish from a menu, and end up with this.

The English poets have always been rather vague about identifying the blooms they are rhapsodising over (cf 'The flowers that bloom in the spring, tra la', or 'The blossom hangs from yonder bough'); in most cases, the ignorant poet had failed to identify the Golden Meadow Thing or, in the latter case, the Climbing Golden Meadow Thing. Some writers have actually done the decent thing and owned up, as in Keats's 'I cannot see what flowers are at my feet', which sounds like a dead cert description of Blind Man's Moustache.

There is a curious lyric by Robert Bridges called 'I Have Loved Flowers that Fade', which suggests a somewhat necrophiliac approach to botany and is thus beyond the scope of this book.

BLIND MAN'S MOUSTACHE

A tiny flower growing deep in meadowland, hedges or anywhere where it is invisible from full standing height. A simple test is to

pass a lawn mower over it; if it is still there afterwards it is Blind Man's Moustache. Not a spectacular bloom as far as size goes, it more than makes up for this in its range of colours (any hue is admissible) and its tenacity, which is probably due to its unpopularity as an ingredient of bunches of wild flowers (it has no stalk).

Widespread on moorlands and hillsides, it can masquerade as grass for years without its disguise being blown. Botanists have always been puzzled by the way it never grows any bigger — for a time there was a theory that it sprang up overnight to three feet and became Greater Hedge Froth. It has now been watched at night, however, and apparently it just becomes invisible.

DOG-EARED MOUSY CHICKENFEED

A small and green plant, it is instantly recognisable for its habit of never being anything but small and green. Close scrutiny will reveal the presence of small green lumps on it. These may be either a) small green buds due to flower next month or b) small green seeds left over from last month's flowering. Nobody has ever been prepared to hang around long enough to find out.

It is possible of course that its flowers are c) small green lumpy flowers.

It grows everywhere all the time.

COMMON OR GARDEN ESCAPE

So called because of its resemblance to a flower growing in profusion in pictures on seed packets. Identification is usually easy because of the tendency to cry, 'Oh, look, it's a tiny version of you know, that thing that Aunty always has in her garden.' If this is followed by the observation that there would still be plenty left if we picked a bunch, that clinches it.

This group also includes vegetable-like things which you are sure you have seen someone on television saying you can cook easily or use raw in salads. Don't. Remember how long it took to get used to spinach?

GLORIOUS HEDGE RAMBLER

Variously called in different parts of the country honeysuckle or dog rose or eglantine or brilliantine, this is a wonderfully colourful flower which grows to six feet but would fall flat on its face if the hedge was not there. When one sees the Glorious Hedge Rambler in all its glory on a summer evening, one cannot help feeling a lump in the throat and a tightness round the heart. Sit down and take it easy. A machine will be along in the morning to flail the hedge until it is nothing but splintered sticks in the ground.

TALL YELLOW PSEUDO-DANDELION

This flower replaces the dandelion and the 476 other flowers identical with the dandelion. In future editions we intend to merge it with the Golden Meadow Thing.

POISONOUS LOATHSOME PRICKLY

Because of its tell-tale habit of stinging, scratching, lacerating, bringing out in bumps, laddering tights, ripping jackets and occasionally killing stone dead but always causing pathological rage and tears, this plant is easy to spot but hard to like. A pity this, as closer acquaintance reveals a mischievous sense of humour on the part of the Poisonous Loathsome Prickly which is quite endearing.

It will, for example, deliberately camouflage itself as Blind Man's Moustache in the middle of a picnic spot or hang down across a path disguised as a tree. It also likes growing at the very height where you intend to pick a handful of Golden Meadow Things. Growing in profusion round stiles, at the only gap in a hedge or at otherwise perfect lavatory spots, it will reach a height of anything between the gap between sock and trouser to bare midriff.

Its distinctive green spikes are invisible.

BIRTHDAY CARD FLOWER

Some blooms are so immediately pretty that the amateur feels it must belong to its own family — what they call violets, primroses, cowslips and so on. This is nonsense; they all fit quite easily into one of the nine previous categories, but it is difficult to resist pressure all the time and so I am creating a special family for the more sentimental reader, i.e. one who has never bought a copy of *The Country Diary of an Edwardian Lady*. Personally, I still regret having to do this; I hate looking at a flower and hearing the words 'For a Very Special Person on his Twenty-First Birthday' floating through my mind.

Section Three

Fungi

There is only one kind of mushroom that the British will ever dare to eat, and there are even fewer when it comes to toadstools. A pity this, as the Continentals are much braver than us about eating wild fungi. They die a lot because of it, of course, but you can't have everything.

Here are the ten basic types.

THE TINY CONTINENTAL DELICACY

This grows in small tins on shelves in delicatessen shops and can be easily spotted through its great expense. It usually likes to grow in the company of palm kernels, crab soup and discontinued lines of Hungarian salad. Instructions for use: read label carefully, glance at price tag and replace on shelf.

THE BUTTON MUSHROOM

This tasteless little fellow, so familiar to us from greengrocers' shops, does not occur in nature. Under EEC regulations, in any case, it will have to be totally replaced by 1987 by the officially-approved Grey Delicious. This does not occur in nature either.

THE DAWN PLUCKED, DEWY FRESH, MEADOW MUSHROOM

The mushroom we all know and love so much. It is very easy to identify, as it grows in dewy fresh meadows and has already been dawn plucked by someone else by the time you get there.

THE TELEGRAPH POLE TOADSTOOL

A large grey fungus, the same size and shape as a long-playing record, which grows forty feet above the ground at the top of dead trees. It is very dangerous; one is enough to cause a broken leg.

THE BRIGHT YELLOW, HIGHLY SUSPICIOUS-LOOKING FUNGUS

One of the most common of all fungi, this sensational-looking glossy monster is highly prized, though nobody is quite sure where. If you should be lucky enough to find one, take it home and cook, then give it to a relative to try.

THE DARK GREY, MILDLY SUSPICIOUS-LOOKING, SLIGHTLY SLIMY FUNGUS

The cheap, paperback version of the previous.

THE ST PAUL'S CATHEDRAL MUSHROOM

Easily identifiable from its large dome. When sliced into thin strips and fried in olive oil with a little marjoram and garlic, it tastes just like veal escalope provençal. It is deadly poisonous.

THE COMMON SHAGPILE CARPET MUSHROOM

This small brown mushroom is found covering the floor of small woods in early autumn. Its drab nondescript appearance makes it one of the least decorative of all fungi; it is, on the other hand, very easy to clean and a brisk going-over with a damp cloth once a fortnight is all that is needed — no need for a vacuum cleaner.

It is perfectly edible; sliced and stewed with a little butter, and a sprinkling of nutmeg or mace, it tastes exactly like little pieces of shagpile carpet sliced and stewed with a little butter.

THE SMALL RED-SPOTTED FAIRYTALE TOADSTOOL

These attractive little fungi grow in the more desirable parts of upper-middle class woods in the Home Counties. They have a tiny door in the stalk, two or more miniature windows upstairs and would suit a couple of gnomes without children on a short let. For further details apply to Potter, Rackham and Uttley, estate agents of Guildford and Dorking, also Mayfair. Absolutely no callers at fungus without an appointment.

THE HOME-ROLLED SLIM PANATELLA MUSHROOM

The legendary mushroom which gives the user powerful hallucinatory visions. It is illegal for this book to describe it, but it is commonly found in most Customs and Excise handbooks. Dried, rolled and smoked, it provides you with the answers to all mankind's problems. Unfortunately, like all universal solutions it has most unpleasant after-effects.

Section Four

Bushes

Bushes have always had a pretty rough deal in nature books. This is not because people dislike them — on the contrary, everyone likes a nice bush, especially if you're a gardener with an awkward gap — but because they occupy a clumsy halfway stage between flowers and trees. They get an after-mention in flower books and they receive grudging appraisal in tree books, but very few books come straight out and say, I am a book about bushes.

Bushes, in fact, are rather like those weights in boxing which are neither glamorously heavy and muscular, nor small and light on their feet, but intermediary like light-welter or semi-demi-featherweight. Or perhaps they are like those showbiz stars who are big enough to appear as guests on other people's shows, but not big enough to have shows of their own. Or maybe like those towns which are too close to London to get their own share of the limelight, such as St Albans, Hatfield, Welwyn Garden City, Hitchin or Basildon. Or even like . . . but you get the idea.

The fact is — and no one ever admits this — the fact is that deep down we all feel that bushes should not exist. There should be *no* halfway stage between flowers and trees, nothing that smells and looks pretty like one, and gets big and strong like the other. There's something, well, a bit *funny* about bushes. They're not gay or anything, but, you know, it's odd that they can't make up their minds what they really are, that's all I'm saying. They marry and have families, *but is their heart really in it?* Still, to show that I'm not prejudiced, unlike other nature guides, I am dividing them into exactly the same number of species as flowers and trees.

35

WAYFARING TREE

Bushes being such a doubtful quantity, the study of them has languished far behind other nature studies. This explains why words appertaining to bushes are often so old-fashioned; whin, for instance, or brake or covert. Or wayfaring. Nobody says wayfaring these days. I'm going wayfaring to Majorca in May. Or, I found this delightful restaurant while wayfaring in Yorkshire.

Nevertheless, we have the wayfaring tree. All this means is a tree that was planted with other trees but travelled a few hundred yards to get away from them and then turned into a bush. They stand by themselves, looking ever so slightly exhibitionist, with bright berries, flowers and other kinds of make-up.

Honestly, I'm as tolerant as the next man, but it does look odd, doesn't it?

SALTY TWISTED STUNTY THING

A sort of leather-jacketed bush that hangs around at the seaside. It is recognisable from its bad posture and tendency to drop one shoulder. You get the impression when you see it that it has a motor cycle parked round the corner, on which it came down that morning from Hatfield or Basildon.

It tends to live on strange-flavoured crisps or savoury rings. At least, packets which have recently contained these are usually found in its spiny, fleshless branches. It is the only known kind of bush which has bad breath.

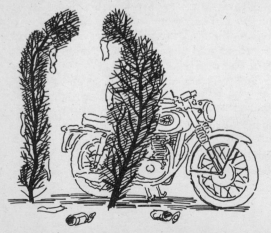

WORMWOOD SHRUBS

Like the previous, but with a criminal record. Gangs of them can be found at otherwise pleasant beauty spots, ensnaring the innocent passer-by and getting them into fierce arguments. They are usually studded with ferocious barbs, hooks, claws and spikes. The *Guardian* would blame this on social deprivation. Personally, I wouldn't, but as I said, this is a tolerant book.

ELDERS AND BETTERS

Some bushes have to suffer the indignity of having their blossoms and fruits wrenched off to convert into home-made wines, though secretly they probably enjoy it. They are instantly recognisable from the heavy sprays of flowers and berries which bedeck them. And from the fact that we use words like 'bedeck' to describe them. They probably wouldn't shrink from words like 'bedizen' or 'guerdon'.

The sad fact about elder bushes is that they are most often found outside cottages leading a sort of double life. Well, as I said, this is a tolerant book, and I only mention it in passing.

Still, and all.

GORSE

Gorse, or furze, or whin, is the only plant that flowers all the year round. If you know the way that nature operates — a short burst of violent activity, followed by a lengthy period of fainting, sighing and insensibility — this makes the gorse suspect immediately. *What does it know that we don't know?*

The answer is, it has a sublime disdain for what people think about it. It produces its yellow flowers and spiky punk thorns all the year round, and just couldn't care less. Whatever it's at, it's at it all the time. No wonder they say: When gorse isn't flowering, kissing's out of fashion.

(I ought to point out, in passing, that kissing is now more in fashion than ever. Almost everyone I meet these days I am forced to kiss on both cheeks, even if I know them perfectly well already. It's all to do with the modern habit of calling strangers by their first name, I think, especially on TV chat shows. Three cheers, then, for Marghanita Laski who was once called Marghanita on 'Any Questions' on Radio 4, and answered: 'My name is Miss Laski!'

Still, perhaps this is beyond the scope of this particular book.)

QUISLING OAK

A quisling oak is any bush that started life as a tree but decided in its teens that it liked life better as a bush and refused to grow any further. You can recognise them from having totally normal tree leaves, but being squat and densely packed with shoots and twigs, rather ostentatiously so. Older readers will probably have the urge to say: Get your hair cut.

Nobody quite knows why this happens. Some scientists think it may be a disease of some kind. Others trace it to an overpowering parent. I think it's just a mild form of transvestism, and if a tree wants to dress up as a bush now and again, well, why not? Just as long as it doesn't go any further.

MUNICIPAL MONSTER

The commonest bush in town parks, Victorian suburbs and driveways up to hotels. It has dark green leaves, a smart turn-out and a slight military air, as if it always wore a great-coat. There is something rather butch about it, to my way of thinking, and I prefer a bush that slops about a bit, but this may say more about me than the bush.

TORQUAY TROPICAL

An odd one, this, which seems to occur only on the promenades of seaside towns in the south, though they are said to have been spotted in the north of Scotland, probably asking for political asylum. The theory is that they can only survive in warm quasi-tropical conditions, though I have only seen them in rainy, wind-swept conditions which seem to have driven off every other bush in sight. They are nature's equivalent of the Italian teenager sent to a language school on the South Coast for the summer and wondering what on earth he is doing there and why he can't pick up local girls.

The bush almost always features palm-like leaves or sword-like spikes, which have usually worn off near the top leaving a bit of trunk like a vulture's neck. No wonder it can't pick up girls.

ORNAMENTAL LABELLED HORTICULTURAL DISPLAY THING

Occurs only in parks, Wisley and the garden of Mr and Mrs Beverley Anstruther, open once a year to the public in aid of a hospital fund. It is heavily made up, far too closely trimmed and even wears a label round its neck, probably the only example of nature going in for fashion accessories. It is excessively pleased with itself, for no discernible reason.

THE LAST REMAINING BUSH

Go up on the moors, past the last house, past the last tree, and there you will see, far out on the lonely expanses, one single, huddled bush all by itself. How brave, you think; what a sturdy little thing to have grown where nobody else dares. How wrong you are — this is the last remaining relic of a forest that used to grow there. It is like the member of a youth gang whom nobody likes, and who looks round one day to say: Hey — where has everyone gone? Don't try to feel sorry for it, or you will be infected by its hopeless introversion and start feeling miserable yourself.

There must have been a reason for a forest to leave it behind. Five million trees can't be wrong.

The main thing to remember is that bushes are all going through a period of adolescence, with all the troubles and traumas that teenagers get. The fact that they are going to remain adolescents all their lives has not dawned on them and probably never will; even if it does, they will deal with it no doubt, just as humans in the same position do.

Section Five

Trees

Trees are the largest and oldest living things, apart from some governors of the BBC, and are generally treated with the awesome respect they deserve, a position from which I will not dissent. A recent survey has shown that trees in areas like the south-east of England have not declined in numbers since the War, as you might expect; if anything, they have increased slightly. Not only are they deserving of respect, they can also look after themselves. What a refreshing change from human society, where everything deserving of respect has to be subsidised.

THE TALL PARK TREE

This large, graceful, imposing tree (which incorporates such previous categories as ash, oak, elm and sycamore) can easily be recognised from its habit of being large, graceful and imposing, except when too many of them stand close together, in which case it stands on tip-toes and looks anorexic. If in doubt, remember that the tall park tree is full of leaves in summer and quite empty in winter, though most practised tree-spotters will know better than to go tree-spotting in winter, when it is impossible to tell most families of trees from the now very common dead tree.

The tall park tree occurs in parkland, where it was placed personally by Capability Brown; in the middle of fields, where it forces tractors to detour; and in large city streets, where it deposits a kind of shiny wax on the cars below.

41

THE FORESTRY COMMISSION TREE

This is a dark green tree invented during the War by a far-sighted government who realised that something would have to be done to cover all those unsightly bare hillsides which disfigure train journeys to the north. They always grow spontaneously in long lines.

They never drop their leaves.

One reason for this is that they have no leaves, only needles.

If a far-sighted government had discovered a use for needles, we would now be a rich nation and not part of the Third World. As it is, the full-grown tree is now cut down and turned into page 3 of the *Sun*, which is presumably not what a far-sighted government had in mind at all, though there was no way that Mr Churchill could have foreseen the arrival of Mr Rupert Murdoch, the well-known immigrant.

The young of the species tends to vanish mysteriously overnight about Dec 21st.

THE RIVERSIDE TREE

Easily spotted, the Riverside Tree always grows at the edge of rivers, where its branches dip gracefully towards the water and stun passing rowers. If you should find a Riverside Tree growing elsewhere, it automatically enters some other category; similarly, any other tree found by the water's edge immediately becomes a Riverside Tree. Classification of trees is nothing if not flexible.

It often grows catkins; there again, often it doesn't.

Curiously, there is no such thing as a Seaside Tree. Anything growing with wood and leaves by the seaside is a Salty Twisted Stunty Thing (see Bushes).

THE CHINESE IMPORT TREE

Many now familiar British trees started life in Himalayan or Chinese forests and would have been well advised to stay there, as they mostly have curiously-shaped leaves which baffle the amateur. It is, however, easily recognised by its totally baffling leaf, which looks like a reject from a kindergarten art class.

Older botanists give the Chinese Import Tree baffling Latin names such as Catalpa or Gingko Biloba, which need not detain us, but which must be very baffling for visitors from China who tend to call them by their real names.

The Chinese Import grows very slowly; some years it seems to shrink a few feet. It also keeps its leaves longer than most trees, partly from a desire to baffle, partly from an atavistic memory of the Chinese seasons.

THE HOLM OAK

The great thing about the holm oak is that it looks nothing like an oak at all, and nobody knows what a holm is. It is probably not even an oak-by-marriage. It is in fact a *trick tree,* along with the sweet chestnut, balsam poplar, mountain ash, hemlock, and all other trees named after plants they did not resemble.

These trick trees are now all holm oaks.

THE CLIMBING TREE

Not, of course, a tree that climbs but one which is good for climbing on. Easily recognisable for its low-hanging branches, or close together boughs or (more rarely) its rope-ladder and tree-house.

Get a child to help you identify it. If he needs a ladder or a hand-up to get started, it is a Tall Park Tree. If he gets stuck halfway up, it is a Forestry Commission Tree. If he never comes back down, it is an enormous beanstalk and beyond the scope of this little book.

THE WEEPING TREE

A misnomer, really, as all trees weep now and then, most commonly about half an hour after it has rained. The true Weeping Tree is more of a sulking tree; it stands with its branches hanging hopelessly in a Gallic expression of disbelief at the awfulness of the world. Any tree which suddenly inspires you with a desire to kick its trunk and

tell it to snap out of it, is a Weeping Tree. Self-pity is bad enough in humans without trees doing it too.

Botanists will tell you that there is also a Handkerchief Tree, and you may wonder if this is connected with the Weeping Tree. Of course not; it is another trick tree (see Holm Oak).

THE MAPLE-SHAPED LEAF TREE

I would like at this point to express my deep gratitude to the Canadian government who, alone among the nations of the world, have had the sense to put a nature lesson on their flag, a single but unmistakable maple leaf. There it stands, or flutters, just one leaf so that we can memorise it and recognise it the next time we see it.

The next time we see it will almost certainly not be on a maple tree, as this is comparatively rare, but on a sycamore, a plane tree, a jar of waffle syrup or, of course, a Canadian flag. The plane tree is the commonest of all the maple-shaped leaf trees, this being a good example of the frog-toad syndrome.

(I ought to explain this, even though it is not made use of in this book. Whenever nature creates something that cannot possibly be confused with something else, it immediately creates something very like it; if nature abhors a vacuum, it simply loathes and hates an unmistakable species. So, there is nothing that can be confused with a frog; except a toad; there is nothing remotely like a rabbit, except a hare; nothing like a butterfly except a moth, nothing like a hedgehog except a porcupine, and so on. Crickets, grasshoppers. Nettles, deadnettles. You name it.

Most nature guides tackle this problem by explaining in minute detail, as there is no other way to do it, the marginal difference between objects caught up in the frog-toad syndrome. This guide treats them as exactly the same species. This is because, if we are told that two similar things are really very different, we will say: 'But

45

NATURE MADE RIDICULOUSLY SIMPLE

they look just the same to me!' If, however, we are told they are just the same, we will begin to notice differences for ourselves. This is the whole principle behind this deeply moral book, though I wasn't going to tell you, and I would rather you forgot all about it.)

THE FRUIT AND NUT TREE

Fruits are nuts, of course, and both are seeds as well, but sex is beyond the scope of this family book, unfortunately. This category merely incorporates all these trees which suddenly develop nuts and fruit about autumn time and are plundered by mothers for Christmas decorations, small boys for conker playing and squirrels for eating. All nuts in Britain are, I'm afraid, basically inedible by humans. This is not because they are impossible to eat, but because the nuts go straight from the green unripe stage to the mouldering, rotten stage, with no stage in between. Remember, too, that it is a law of nature that the brighter and more attractive a fruit looks, the less edible it is.

THE EPONYMOUS TREE

Are you fed up with smarty-pants journalists using the word 'eponymous'? I sure am. *Gandhi*, with Ben Kingsley in the eponymous role. The other day I caught myself saying, '*Breakfast at Tiffany's*, with Audrey Hepburn eating the eponymous rolls.' Then I knew it had gone too far.

But there seems no other way of describing the Wellingtonias, Lawsonias and Leylandias which droop, green and huge, across the more haut-bourgeois parts of our landscape. Who is Lawson? Can it be the same Leyland? Why a Wellingtonia and no Napoleonia? How, more important, to distinguish between them?

I don't think, frankly, there is any need to. I call them all Kingtonias. I think you should do the same. Adapt your own surname, I mean. If Forsyth can get away with forsythia, and Dahl with dahlia, the world is ready for the smithia and jonesia. If you have trouble with your surname, drop me a line or call in at my publishers — it's the one with the small, stunted hamish-hamiltonia outside the front door.

Section Six

Birds

THE BROWN HEDGE BIRD

This brown bird which lives in hedges, or perhaps this bird which lives in brown hedges, or often both, is a master of camouflage and can usually only be seen flying at high speeds between two hedges. This would enable it to evade its enemies if it had any; as it is, no other creature in nature seems at all interested in its existence. Perhaps its evasive behaviour is based on shame at its own drab appearance. It is by far the most common and the most boring bird in Britain, and its song comes to match, being a single toot or tweet, like a clarinettist on lesson one. It is very good at not catching breadcrumbs in mid-air.

THE MUCH LOVED GARDEN BIRD

Many amateurs still think that when birds sing and hop around, they are being merry and affectionate. They are not, of course; they are being aggressive and demanding the price of a cup of coffee. As, however, human beings are soft at heart and in the head, I suppose we shall go on regarding this thing as a much loved garden bird, even when it beats on the window with its beak and tells you to get that goddam food out on the bird table, or else. It is the equivalent of the Birthday Card Flower.

N.B. Although not strictly speaking a bird, it is worth noting the existence of that legendary fowl, the Paperback Bird. This family includes all birds beginning with P, such as Penguin, Puffin, Pelican, Kestrel, etc. It is without doubt the most tasteful bird in Britain, being daring sometimes but never going too far. Clad in orange or green or blue, it feeds off hardback publishers, and is usually harmless — sometimes it runs into difficulties and has to be helped. Even when boring you can't help liking it and most families keep a few as pets around the house.

THE FLOCK OF PETER SCOTTS

Peter Scotts, which always come in flocks of 17,000, can only be seen at dusk outlined against the sunset, which only comes in orange. It only has two parts of the body, the neck and wings. Its harsh call can best be transcribed as: 'Paint-me, paint-me.'

THE GREAT, BIG, WHITE, FAT, EVIL-EYED SEABIRD

Britain's only known seabird, it wheels overhead at the seaside uttering harsh caustic comments on the immature state of one's suntan and the unfashionable nature of one's swimwear. It flees inland during what it thinks of as bad weather, i.e. when the wind goes over Force One or when waves appear on the calm sea.

No longer able to catch fish, it now feeds off municipal rubbish dumps and is the only known bird with bad breath. Despite this, it always looks inexplicably pleased with itself.

There is an inland version of this bird which behaves in exactly the same way, but is known as the Great, Big, Black, Fat, Evil-eyed Landbird.

THE V-SHAPED ROCKET

Locally called swift, swallow or martin, this is the principal visitor to our shores during the summer and flies overhead at speeds in excess of 300 mph, twittering faintly, as well it might. It travels far too fast to be identified, which is how it can be easily identified. Like the much rarer RAF combat plane, which it closely resembles, it disappears at the end of September.

THE RARE-TO-MIDDLING BIRD OF PASSAGE

Not normally a resident of Britain, this nondescript creature very occasionally spends a bargain break weekend at Romney Marsh, Blythburgh Estuary and other places over-run by the ubiquitous photographer. Scared by the rough, raucous behaviour of this lesser spotter, it usually cuts its weekend short and flies back to wherever it came from, probably the *Observer Magazine.*

THE INVISIBLE SONGBIRD

Carolling joyfully, the invisible songbird sits at the top of a tree and trills a message of pure pleasure. The listener, if he is anything like me, reacts with feelings of happiness, serenity, perplexity, irritation and finally sheer paranoid fury as he fails to spot the presence of the songster anywhere in the tree. The songbird, which has the unusual ability to throw its voice, is of course in the next tree.

THE WELL-HUNG GAME BIRD

This gaily-plumaged bird lives behind the windows of better-class butchers and poulterers in Knightsbridge and other country towns. Hanging in tidy rows, it sheds its feathers after a few days to reveal a scrawny body containing 7,153 tiny bones, five lead pellets and $1\frac{1}{3}$ oz of meat. It is not known to make any noise.

THE CROSSWORD BIRD

A surprisingly common bird which nests in the smaller crevices of upper-class crosswords. The most common members of this family are the auk, tern, moa, gled, cob and erne.

Oddly, this family also contains all Britain's night birds — bat, owl, jar, etc.

THE MOTORWAY HAWK

The only remaining bird of prey in Britain, the motorway hawk can be seen beside motorways hovering at about forty feet above the hard shoulder. Motionless, apart from its flapping wings, it has its steely eyes fixed on some hapless prey in the grass below. Relentlessly, it focuses all its will on the target. Inevitably, the hapless prey spots the wildly-flapping wings and slips away laughing to itself. Disappointed, the hawk sideslips and starts hovering again. Lord knows when it ever gets to eat.

Many drivers on motorways find the sight of the hovering bird a fascinating one and, transfixed, drive gently through the central reservation and out the other side.

Section Seven

Insects with Wings
or Things That Refuse To Fly Straight

Nature is justly famed for inventing things long before man, or even Leonardo da Vinci, got round to it, but this chapter will reveal to us the full glory. of nature's ingenuity, coming up with everything from dice games to airline luggage. All that man has invented in the insect field is insect spray. It sometimes makes one modest to be human.

FIRST WORLD WAR FLYING MACHINES

The biplane was invented just before the First World War and discontinued shortly afterwards, presumably because of its lack of speed or because passengers hated sitting under a wing as well as on top of one, but it has always been present in nature as the one-seater Dragonfly or Damselfly. On summer days this pleasant little flying craft can be spotted out on reconnaissance missions over enemy lines. It probably cannot see or take aerial photographs very well, but its hearing is remarkable; you only have to say, 'Hey, look at the drag . . .' and it vanishes.

Incidentally, lack of speed might be rather useful in modern aeroplanes. Advanced defence systems are all programmed to spot something fast approaching; a biplane would probably get through without being challenged. Still, this is beyond the scope of the present book.

The First World War Flying Machine Insect is actually more advanced than any aeroplane in one respect; it can step up production fast and cheaply by breeding. Its mating ritual is so private that it can only be seen on television.

THE FLYING SUITCASE BEETLE

Shiny, hard-backed luggage has recently become popular for travellers who have to protect themselves against that terrible predator, the airport employee. The same device was invented millions of years ago by the beetle to protect himself against birds. In fact, the beetle is in the position of a traveller *who actually gets inside his own luggage* for protection. Will things ever get so bad at Heathrow that we have to do the same? One hopes not.

Nature, of course, is still ahead of the game. We may think that the beetle has a design fault when we see it lying on its back, apparently unable to right itself, but before we laugh we ought to think what trouble we too would have locked in our own suitcase. It is the beetle that has the last laugh, though. With a convulsive click it can leap in the air and land the right way up. When I see my suitcase tossed this way and that, with the duty-free being pounded to bits inside, I wish mine could do the same.

In addition, the flying suitcase beetle is able to home back to base through some sort of inbuilt radar that we do not yet fully comprehend. My suitcase shows more talent for going to Amsterdam.

SINGLE SEAT FIGHTERS

This seems the best description for those small flying insects which can fly and sting. Nature, again, has come up trumps by inventing aerial warfare long before man even thought of throwing stones at each other. The only thing that nature has not bothered to invent is the equivalent of baling out by parachute, but when you have as many aircraft in the air as nature does, it doesn't make economic sense to worry about repairs and rescue work.

People who like identifying aircraft will enjoy spotting the different kinds of fighting insect. There is the Wasp, for instance, which will

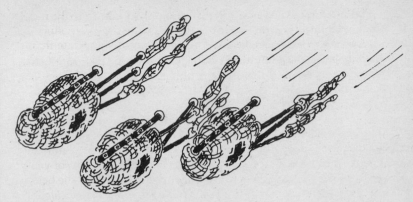

attack everything living; the Bee, which refuels in mid-air from flowers but possesses only a one-strike retaliatory firepower; the Kamikaze Ant, which flies only one mission and then dies after mating in mid-air (unlike our gallant World War II pilots, who mated first and then died in mid-air); and the Mosquito, which refuels in mid-air from man.

The Mosquito, incidentally, is the only one so far as I know which makes a noise while flying. It is a high-pitched whine which cuts out abruptly before an attack on the enemy. Hitler copied this during the War, but could not call his device the Mosquito, as the British Patent Laws are very strict about this sort of name-stealing, so it became the Doodle-bug. Why doodle-bug, though? The German for bagpipe is Dudelsack. Did Hitler perhaps think of his weapon as a sort of flying pibroch? We shall never know. The subject, in any case, is somewhat beyond the scope of this book.

NIGHT RECONNAISSANCE FLIERS

Naturalists get very cross when beginners classify bats with birds, simply because bats can fly. I see their point. But then I get very cross when naturalists proceed to classify bats with dolphins and dogs, simply because they have a similar warm-blooded family background. The crucial thing about the bat is that *it flies crooked* and is therefore closer to a lot of insects. For me, a bat is a flying insect and I will not budge from this position.

Flying crooked is the one great invention of nature that human flying has hardly even started to copy, and yet if nuclear-armed missiles flew like anything mentioned in this chapter — dodging and crouching, weaving and bobbing — they would be unstoppable. This, too, is beyond the scope of this book, but I wish someone would do something about it.

THE FLYING DICE

Another mystery which has bothered naturalists is why so-called ladybirds, of all crooked flying things, should be the only ones with clear markings like some Third World air force — bright colours and squadron recognition dots. It seems to have occurred to none of them that this was nature's great attempt to create an in-flight dice and board game. 'Look, I've thrown a two-spot!' you can hear nature almost saying.

You can certainly hear me say it sometimes. I once spent a happy afternoon in the Chilterns with some friends and a bottle of wine, playing Throw The Ladybird. I stood to win £50 in the final round and the only man who could beat me had to throw a seven-spot to creep ahead of me and scoop the jackpot. That is, unfortunately, exactly what he did.

There is, however, no such thing as a seven-spot ladybird in nature. When we looked closer, we found that the unscrupulous wretch had secretly painted an extra blob on a six-spot.

It is sad that a lust for money should interfere with natural selection.

AIR STEWARDESSES

There is a kind of flying insect which is so ethereal, so transiently beautiful, that it cannot bear to grow old, and dies within twenty-four hours. It is sometimes referred to as the May Fly. I compare it privately to Ilse, an air stewardess I once met on a Lufthansa flight. Oh, Ilse, how perfect you were, how utterly devastating! Did you live long enough to hand out earphones on another flight, I wonder? If you did, could I have my Jack Higgins paperback back some time, please?

THE CLOUD INSECT

An insect which always flies round in clouds. A cloud of gnats, we say, or a cloud of midges. It is always the same insect, so small that it cannot even be seen unless forming a cloud. I am always reminded, when watching them, of standing on the Sussex Downs in those terrible days in 1941 and watching the clouds of Spitfires and Messerschmitts far above me. Oddly enough, the other day I was watching a cloud of midges in my garden only two feet away, when one of them startled me by pulling out in a plume of smoke and falling to the ground at my feet, a burnt-out wreck. Amazed, I bent to have a closer look. It was a cigarette end thrown from next door.

TINY CRAWLY THINGS ON LEAVES

These can be easily recognised by the fact that if you stick around for a couple of weeks watching them closely, they will suddenly turn into butterflies or other winged insects when you have taken your eyes off them for a moment, and fly off before you look back. When touched, they roll up into a tight ball. If this is their idea of avoiding being eaten, they are going about it the wrong way.

Some of these so-called caterpillars are very hairy. Some are very smooth. Some have tiny drooping sales rep moustaches.

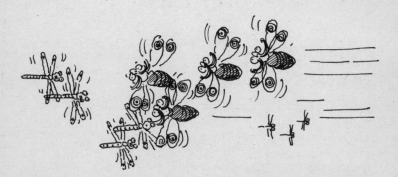

THE DIRECTIONLESS, UNARMED, MULTI-COLOURED DECOY

The great family of butterflies and moths can be recognised by their habit of flying *so* crooked that they even deceive themselves and always land on a place they were not aiming at. They spend the next few minutes in silent thought, trying to work out where they are and then trying to look as if they meant to be there all along.

The fact is that nature created this charming creature simply as an experiment to see how far evasive flight could be taken. It now knows the answer: too far. There is nothing in nature which can fly crooked enough to *catch* a butterfly. What this means is that nature has created a weapons system which can never be stopped and can never hit the target. It is a humbling thought.

It also means that if butterflies flew straight, they would now be extinct. Perhaps there used to be a great family of straight-flying butterflies which *did* become extinct.

FLY

Anything not contained in the above is a fly.

Section Eight

Creepy Crawlies
or The Slime Factor

One of the major breakthroughs of this book is the abandonment of the theory that everything in nature is nice.

Now, to the specialist everything is fascinating. The flea expert is as keen on fleas as the elephantologist is on elephants. Wild flower books never ever use the word 'weed', and no nature book ever refers to anything as a 'pest'. That is why naturalists are the total opposite of farmers, who regard almost the whole of nature as a personal enemy, and sometimes seem hell-bent on stamping it out.

Like most people's, my position is somewhere between the two. I regard nature as fascinating, if confusing, but I draw the line at slimy things, which I regard as slimy. So I have to admit that I wrote this section feeling slightly ill throughout. I hope it doesn't show too much, because I am sure there are people who find slugs friendly little creatures, and they are welcome.

NASTY, SLIMY THINGS

Also known as slugs, these friendly little creatures are so embarrassed by their revolting appearance and abominable texture that they like to hide in dark corners or in the middle of old tree stumps where nobody can see them. The only thing that makes them different at all from half-chewed liquorice is the presence of tiny antennae which wave about like someone trying to get Channel 4. They have many enemies in nature, among whom I am proud to number myself.

If I ever get into *Who's Who*, I will list slug-culling as my hobby.

SLIMY THINGS WHICH HAVE HAD THE DECENCY TO GROW A SHELL

These are generally known as snails when creeping wild and as escargots when lying still in a restaurant. Their sense of camouflage is so uniquely bad in nature that they leave long silvery trails behind them, which thrushes can walk along till they find the snails at the end and eat them.

The theory behind their presence in restaurants is that they have a lovely delicate flavour of garlic, butter and parsley, but in my experience this comes simply from adding parsley, garlic and butter. If you eat snails without the added delicacies, you are in for a nasty shock. That is why I admire thrushes so much.

TINY, SLIMY THINGS WHICH WRITHE AROUND A LOT IN OLD TOBACCO TINS

Their natural enemy is the angler, who calls them maggots. He exterminates them by putting a hook through them and dangling them in a river until a fish comes along and finishes them off. It may seem cruel to disembowel, drown *and* eat alive a living creature, and it is, so I can only assume that the angler hates them very much indeed. Certainly, he never pretends that the maggot secretly enjoys the whole thing.

Sometimes the fish unfortunately gets caught on the hook as well, in which case the angler will extricate him and return him to the water as quickly as possible. It is the maggot he hates, not the fish. Well, I know how he feels.

SMALL BUT LONGISH SLIMY THINGS

It is sometimes assumed that Charles Darwin spent his whole life studying evolution, but in fact he spent many long years studying worms and coming to the conclusion that the action of worms on the soil was the best possible thing that could happen to it. This being so, I shall say nothing against them for the time being.

However, Darwin's theories are coming in for a lot of questioning and readjustment these days (something to do with his centenary celebrations, I think), so I reserve the right to dislike worms just in case they turn out to be anti-social after all.

LARGE, LONG SLIMY THINGS

Snakes are not in fact slimy, as anyone who has ever dandled a snake on his knee will testify, and this once happened to me in Whipsnade Junior Zoo, an experience which I never thought would come in useful. Most sensible people, however, would rather run a mile than do something as crazy as dandle a snake on their knee.

That, actually, is how you recognise these charming friendly creatures — through your impulse to run a mile, an instinct as deep-seated as our urge to feel pleasure at the sight of a rainbow or to turn round and stare when someone shouts 'Duck!'. Don't forget, though, that all snakes have an impulse to get as far away as possible when they see human beings, having a deep-seated instinctive loathing of large, non-slimy, two-legged things.

This seems a satisfactory arrangement all round, and dandling on knees by either side can only serve to damage our mutual respectful distrust.

THE LONG-LEGGED DADDY

The only flying creature whose legs are longer than its wings. Naturalists are baffled as to why this should be so. It seems pretty obvious to me; it is a deterrent. When its natural enemies start eating it, they give up in disgust after the first tasteless, meatless leg and let it go. Better lose a leg than lose everything.

SMALL SQUIDGY THINGS ON THE GROUND

If you find any otherwise unidentifiable squashy object on the ground, rest assured that it is merely awaiting the moment to grow legs and wings and fly away. This is sometimes described as a miracle of nature, and if by this is meant that it is miraculous they are not stepped on before take-off, then I suppose this is true.

This transition from total dormancy to complete airborneness may seem a strange way of developing a flying object, but after all humans do it exactly the same way. Our flying objects can lie around at the developmental stage for years on end, then very often get totally cancelled. However, the reasons for this are beyond the scope of this little book.

THE KENNETH ALLSOP BUG

It was from Kenneth Allsop, the late lamented, that I learnt about the bug that lives only in the back of colour TV sets in New York, living on the juices from the transistors or something like that. Apparently it could not live anywhere else. Where it had been living until John Logie Baird came along, I have no idea. But by extension there must also be organisms that live only in transistor radios (stone deaf), in electric toasters (immune to heat) and hair driers (able to hang on in very high winds). More research needs to be done, though not by me.

Observant readers may notice that this section, unlike all the others, contains only eight basic species. I am sorry. I was feeling rather nauseous by the end. I had to stop short. I hope readers will understand.

Section Nine

Animals

Four-legged wild life in Britain used to be much more impressive than it is now, with our great forests being freely roamed by wild boars, sabre-toothed tigers, mammoths, wild deer, dragons and so on. This came abruptly to an end at a date variously given as the end of the Middle Ages, the discovery of the gun or the beginning of the Waverley Novels. The main cause was the disappearance of our great forests, which were ravaged by greedy timber wolves, and by printers looking for enough paper for Sir Walter Scott's prodigious output.

Of the larger animals, only the deer is left. The smaller ones have survived because nobody thought they were worth hunting, though in the absence of anything bigger they have suddenly become desirable, just as mews cottages, once stablemen's living quarters, are now desirable middle-class homes. This, however, is slightly outside the scope of this book.

DEER

There are two distinct types of deer: Parkland Deer and Royal Stag Hunt Outrage Deer.

Parkland deer are instantly recognisable, as they pose with considerable grace and tactical skill under trees in parks so as to present their best profiles to photographers and members of the National Trust. It is not often realised that the deer are taken in by convoys of trucks each night and replaced again each morning by deer wardens; this is always done before the park is re-opened to visitors. When herds grow thin, their numbers are sometimes bolstered by lifelike but artificial silhouette imitations; there is at least one stately home in Wiltshire where all the deer are now cardboard cutouts, and very effective they are too.

Royal Stag Hunt Outrage Deer live wild on the Scottish hills, where occasionally they are culled in a burst of gunfire from members of the Royal Family, which is usually enough to crowd everyone except Ian Botham off the front pages of the nationals. Critics who object to this sort of thing should remember that all royal families, too, have over the years been culled by assassination, bombing, execution or being married to Kaiser Wilhelm, so for them it is the only way of life they know and they see nothing odd about it.

FOXES

Foxes have survived the increasingly hostile countryside by moving en masse to Bristol, where they parade outrageously in an attempt to get into films made by the BBC Natural History Unit. It is almost impossible for some members of the BBC to get to work without being waylaid by foxes striking provocative poses, demonstrating their skill at unarmed combat or even waving scripts in front of their eyes. It is even reported that some over-theatrical foxes have taken to wearing eye-shadow and mincing through the outskirts of an evening. One shaken producer at the BBC swears that he was propositioned by a big butch fox the other day, but he has now gone on leave due to overwork.

ANIMALS YOU PROBABLY THOUGHT WERE SAFELY DOMESTICATED

Some animals normally found in the home are also found in a totally wild state, such as Alsatians on building sites and the legendary East Anglian hamster. But the only one you are likely to see is the wild pony, an intelligent creature which fails to see the point in having a man on its back.

I was talking recently to a Dartmoor farmer who had tried to cultivate wild ponies for the purpose of pony-trekking, but with little success; his guests soon got bored with trekking long distances on foot just to have a look at a few wild ponies which ran away. Next year he intends to turn his land over for cultivation as that old Dartmoor speciality, a rifle range; he has written to several military leaders and has already received a favourable response from Colonel Gaddafy.

Faced with the problem of what to do with the pony population, he has decided on an intervening year of pony-hunting and pony-shooting. This will only shock people who do not know farmers well. See the section on Your Fellow Two-legged Country-lovers.

CAMELS

Camels, after being scarce for many years in Britain, are now found in many places though not as many as I would like. In their absence, I tend to go for Lucky Strike.

ANIMALS THAT MOVE VERY SLOWLY UNDER ROADS

Badgers and moles, chiefly. The conventional way of distinguishing between them is based on the supposed fact that one is large and white and the other is small and black. If we ever got to see them this might be useful but we don't and it isn't.

No, the main difference between them is that people feel kindly inclined towards badgers but not towards moles. Anything but. (Very odd, as badgers are surly beasts and moles totally inoffensive.) This explains the fact that when a new motorway cuts across a badger path, the authorities always have to spend an extra million pounds putting a badger tunnel under the roadway. Moles don't get tunnels; they get sticks of dynamite put in their molehills.

This is also very odd, as moles don't live under molehills, which are merely rubbish dumps left behind after they have dug tunnels for food collection. In fact, moles don't really live underground at all, they just feed there. But farmers attack their feeding arrangements so fiercely that moles have nowhere left to go much, except under motorways. This, I feel convinced, is why so many of our major motorways are crumbling — they are being undermined by hungry moles. If we left out food for moles instead of dynamite, we might reduce our motorway maintenance expenditure at a stroke and save all the money spent building badger tunnels.

I can see, though, that this subject may be outside the scope of the present volume.

ESCAPES FROM FARMS, CIRCUSES AND TV COMMERCIALS

Some parts of the country have been almost entirely overrun by animals which have moved out of captivity into more spacious accommodation. They are variously referred to as coypus, pumas, llamas, vicunas and that telly gorilla, but most of them are probably only minks. It takes practice to recognise them, but any animal which brings David Attenborough to mind or which gives you the urge to say, 'Excuse me, but haven't I seen you on television somewhere?' is almost certainly an escapee, unless it is Willy Rushton.

ANIMALS THAT MOVE VERY SLOWLY ACROSS ROADS

The squashed hedgehog became the cult animal of the 1970s and early '80s, featuring in more cartoons than any other kind of wild life and being largely responsible for the major success of 'Not The Nine O'Clock News'. It seems to be on the decrease now, either because it is genuinely on the decrease, or because the survivors have learnt to use foot-bridges.

ANIMALS THAT MOVE VERY FAST ACROSS ROADS

There is no point in trying to distinguish between stoats, ferrets, weasels, ermines and so on. They move too fast. With their razor-sharp teeth they can slash through a motor car tyre in five seconds or sever a petrol pipe, and are thus in my view a major factor for road safety.

LITTLE FOUR-LEGGED ANIMALS THAT
MAKE YOU GO 'AH!'

Into this category come all the animals like field mice, rabbits, squirrels and frogs.

LITTLE FOUR-LEGGED ANIMALS THAT
MAKE YOU GO 'UGH!'

And into this one go all the others, like voles, shrews, rats, and toads.

66

Section Ten

Insects with No Wings But a Lot of Legs

Any ordinary book on wild life will tell you that insects are strictly limited to things with only six legs, of which there are about a million species (or 6,000,000 legs in all). This is plainly ridiculous; it would theoretically be possible to look at a million insects one after the other and not find two the same.

If you have grasped the principles contained in this book, you will see at once that the variation of species is far too large and must be reduced by 5,999,990, and that the restrictions on legs is far too strict. So let us start again and get it over with comparatively quickly.

SEXIPEDE

A six-legged insect. The back pair of legs is used for power, the middle pair for steering and the front pair for cleaning each other.

OCTOPEDE

The extra pair of legs owned by an octopede is needed to take victims out of its web so that they can be filleted, beaten flat with a twig and cut into bite-size portions.

FOURTEENOPEDE

Basically, an octopede with fitted seat belts. Economical, good about town and easy to clean. The most familiar model on British roads is the Woodlouse. Its fourteen legs and plated panels give it a right to be marketed as a Crustacean.

CENTIPEDE

As its Latin name suggests, it has about thirty legs. In regular models there are fifteen on one side and fifteen on the other, though you may meet customised one-offs with a different arrangement.

MILLIPEDE

An insect with seventy legs, thirty-five on one side and the same on the other. You would expect it to move the thirty-five on one side, then the thirty-five on the other side and so on. You would be wrong. If it did that, it would fall over the whole time. It tends more to phase the use of its legs in waves, like a badly-trained peasant guerrilla army in TV newsclips.

BILLIPEDE

A billipede has so many legs (about 130) that the back part of its body tends to catch up the front part, through sheer nervousness at being so far from the command centre. Occasionally it panics and tramples itself to death.

JITTERBUG

One of the above, but wriggling around so much it is impossible to count its legs.

ZILLIPEDE

The most-legged insect known so far, with about 95 on either side, or a grand total of roughly 190. The front bit has sometimes been known to curl up for the night's sleep while the back part is still marching into camp, tired and hungry. Being so long, it is capable of coming across a strange insect in the bush and attacking it, before realising that it is biting its own hinder parts. For this reason, it normally sits and waits for any doubtful insect to go past, like a car waiting for a train at a level crossing, in case it is looking at itself.

STAMPEDE

More than one of the above.

PALINDROME

A curious creature which, if spelt backwards, reads emordnilap.

Section Eleven

Things That Can Swim A Width Underwater
or
Probably, But Not Necessarily, Fish

This section deals only with freshwater swimming things. For saltwater things, consult your fishmonger. He will point silently to the chart hanging on his wall. This doesn't mean that he wants you to buy it, though after ten minutes free study I would offer to pay a small continuation fee.

SALMON

We had better get the salmon over with first, as it has the most complicated life-cycle of all forms of marine life, or at least the most crowded engagement diary. It visits more places and undergoes more changes of name than an urban terrorist; I don't know a great deal about jackals, but I suspect that Carlos the Salmon would have been a much more accurate sobriquet.

The salmon starts life as an egg in the heart of beautiful Scotland, among the burns and heather of old Scotia (see the *Oxford Book of Scottish Tourist Verse* passim). When old enough to swim a few lengths, it goes downstream to the sea, being known at this stage as an elver, which is confusing, as this is really a baby eel. But everything is confusing for the salmon just now; not only must it make the transition from fresh to sea water and change altitude by several thousand feet — during its life the salmon goes higher than most birds — but it will also find that folk on the east coast of Scotland speak with a very different accent.

In the ocean it undergoes initiation ceremonies such as buzzing oil rigs, visiting Norway and going halfway round the world, briefly becoming a herring. Then, driven by some unfathomable instinct which we do not at present fully understand, it goes all the way back up the same river, or one very like it, just in time to inaugurate the Scottish tourist season and lay its eggs (or salmon mousse) at the head of the river. It then returns to the sea for a special final farewell appearance, only to return a few months later to spend the rest of its life in a small underwater granny flat beneath a stone, where it is called upon to do a lot of egg-sitting. It ends its life as a side of best Scotch smoked.

It can be easily recognised by the frantic, hunted look in its eyes which it does not lose even on the fishmonger's slab.

STICKLEBACK (DoE)

The stickleback is a small educational fish which is bred in large quantities by the Department of Education and released into streams all over Britain during revision time for Biology 'O' Levels. It is the only fish which will stay still long enough to be drawn in good detail.

JELLIED EELS

A kind of underwater snake, the eel secretes a jelly which enables it to swim smoothly through the water. It is only found in the East End of London and is quite inedible.

COARSE FISH

Variously known as dace, roach, chubb, yale, squire, etc, the coarse fish has a rough, boisterous sense of humour and likes being thrown back in the water, for which purpose it will climb again and again on to anything dangled into its habitat. It is ideal for the purpose, being made of some rough, canvas-like material, which is not only hard-wearing but waterproof, and inedible. Variously known as brill, fab, ace, gear, it is easily recognised for its bluff habits of winking at the observer, pulling faces and sticking its tongue out. Also known as smelt, kilt, whelp, skalp and fart, it is the only fish known to pick its nose.

CROCODILE

More familiar to us as the half-submerged log in African rivers, or at least in films about African rivers, crocodiles in Britain never grow longer than six inches and resemble half-submerged twigs. With one chomp from its mighty but tiny jaws, it can draw blood from a little finger or nip a toe quite badly.

They are not native to these shores, but are escapes from British crocodile farms, where they are bred for the manufacture of crocodile skin contact lens-holders. Marinated and baked in a slow oven they make delightful if chewy cocktail snacks. (But remember to remove the contact lenses first.)

HEAVIER-THAN-AIR INSECTS, BIRDS, ANIMALS, ETC.

These are not strictly speaking fish. In fact, they are not fish at all, any more than a flying fish is a bird. Still, you may very well during your underwater observations see one flash past and it is as well to remember that, however surprised *you* may be to see a duck or otter swim past, you are going to give him a heart attack as well.

TROUT IN A FARM

The trout is now an endangered and protected species, and may only be grown on a farm. Trout have taken surprisingly well to being turned out into farm fields, and may often be seen browsing contentedly all day on the wet grass, flicking with their tails to keep the flies away. Trout milk is rich, but the yield is low.

SCAMPI OUT OF A BASKET

One of the three most tiresome conversations you ever hear in a restaurant, fish shops or indeed at the water's edge is whether this thing looking like a prawn (the only creature whose moustache is the largest part of its anatomy) is actually a shrimp, langoustine, crayfish, Norwegian lobster or scampi. What does it matter? They all taste the same, thanks to the cocktail dressing or creamy sauce in which it meets its death by drowning. Personally, I'd go for the champignons à la Grecque or the smoked mackerel but *not* the sweetbreads.

The second most tiresome conversation in restaurants is about which animal sweetbreads come from, and from which part of that animal.

The third tiresome conversation centres on what is the singular form of the word scampi.

The singular of scampi is shrimpo.

FISH FINGER

The life cycle of the fish finger is still little understood, but it seems to start as a tiny rectangle no larger than a fingernail, and coloured grey. It feeds on breadcrumbs. When it has reached its maximum length of four inches it turns the familiar golden-orange colour and creeps into a box to breed and die.

WHITEBAIT

Any fish that does not correspond to one of the above can be classified as whitebait, which is the commonest fish in Britain apart from scampi. It is scheduled to be replaced throughout the EEC before 1988 by greybait, which is already widely sold in fish and chip shops in Britain under the name of cod, rock, plaice, haddock, etc.

Section Twelve

Hovercreatures

LONG-LEGGED WATERBOATMAN

See, skimming across the pond or river, the skilful long-legged waterboatman, steering his way instinctively between obstacles and avoiding the predatory bird or fish which is ever on the watchout to snap him up. He knows these waters well, and his apparently clumsy movements belie his devotion to the water.

WEEKEND WATERBOATPERSON

See, skimming across the river or pond, this gaily-coloured creature, bumping into every obstacle and knocking over half the other insects he meets. This is the weekend waterboatperson, a pretentious little creature which only gets on the water one weekend in four and is a complete menace to the local residents, being quite unskilled in navigation and never properly equipped. Sometimes they are swept helplessly out to sea, but not often enough.

POWER WATERBOATPERSON

Hear, skimming across the luckless pond or river, this noisy but exceptionally speedy little water bug. See him terrify any other kind of water life in his path and cut slower hovercreatures in two. Watch him hit the far bank and disintegrate into a thousand pieces.

AIR/SEA RESCUE WATERBOATMAN

Sometimes you will be lucky enough to see a gangly kind of flying insect drop down slowly from a height of ten feet, manoeuvring somewhat like a helicopter, i.e. clumsily and painfully. He has spotted an insect in difficulties on the water surface below. With infinite care he judges the wind currents just right, so that he lands by the struggling victim and rescues him from a watery grave. He then eats him.

LONE ROUND-THE-WORLD WATERBOATPERSON

As you watch the busy traffic buzzing its way across any river or stream, going to and fro between the banks or rocks, you will sometimes spot a hovercreature determinedly going *along* the stream and showing no intention of landing on either bank. The only possible explanation, scientists now believe, is that he is going round the world. Good luck, lad.

HOUSEWATERBOATPERSON

Some hovercreatures stay exactly where they are, all day long, certainly longer than the average user of this book can be bothered to wait and watch. This is because they actually live there, rather like someone on a houseboat on the Thames by Chiswick. How they eat is somewhat uncertain, but presumably their mate has gone ashore to get milk and bread, got waylaid by a friend and gone to join him in an unattended gin and tonic.

I C B BOATMAN

Another hovercreature that enlivens the busy water scene on pond or river, canal or stream, is the fast-flying little creature that you occasionally see going past at tremendous speed just above the water surface, never landing, never stopping and never reappearing. This is the intercontinental ballistic boatman, who is on a search-

and-destroy mission alert 24 hours round the clock, night and day.
So far, thank God, one has never gone off, but you can sometimes see
holes in river banks which show how great the impact of even an
unexploded I C B boatman is.

HOLIDAY WATERBOATMAN

A relative of the weekend waterboatperson, this hovercreature appears
only during the summer and goes along the rivers of England
bumping into the bank every two inches, and pushing off backwards.
It leaves a trail of litter behind it.

BALACLAVA WATERBOATMAN

Also known as the SAS riverthug, this terrifying and deadly
hovercreature lurks invisibly on the surface of the water, then
dashes ashore to capture some helpless victim and drags it off to kill
it. Sometimes it just plays with the victim, in its so-called interrogation
ritual, but after that it kills it anyway.

SEALINKSECT

If you are an insect that cannot fly, swim or hover, and you want to get across a piece of water, what do you do? Yes, you can walk round it, but what if it is a stream or river? Yes, you can jump on a twig and float to the other side, but what if there isn't a twig available? Well, you jump on the Sealinksect, or ferryboatman, which plies incessantly from bank to bank.

Unfortunately, there are very few insects who actually want to get from bank to bank. That is why the Sealinksect is doing such poor business, even in the summer months, and will almost certainly become extinct in a few years. Nature is not only red in tooth and claw, it is also pretty hard on the obsolete investment.

Section Thirteen

Basic Geology

Geology is that branch of natural history which claims that everything beneath our feet is either igneous or non-igneous rock. In other words, it is the only science which tries to divide nature into smoking and non-smoking compartments. It does this by using the following two phrases at every possible opportunity:

'These rocks were formed at a time of upheaval in the earth's crust, and under immense pressure were buckled, twisted and turned on end to form the rather complex land formation we have today.'

'These rocks were laid down over millions of years by the deposit of tiny sea creatures at the bottom of lakes on the site of the British Isles, and have since been overlaid by other deposits to form the rather complex land formation we have today.'

Geologists, in other words, get very excited over what happened billions of years ago and seem incredibly bored by the evidence left lying around today, rather like a gardener who says: 'You really should have been here last week when the garden was looking wonderful — I'm afraid it's a mess today.'

To hide this boredom, they have resorted to several tricks to get the outsider interested. For a start, they call everything rocks, even when it's clearly only sand or soggy clay. Then they colour their geological maps in stunning bright poster paints and slash them across the country in wonderful shapes. They give exciting or poetic names to their rocks, such as boulder clay, millstone grit, or lower green-sands. And they print exciting time charts, with cross headings

like: 'Cretaceous Era — great lakes form over Britain — millions of
sea creatures deposited — invention of the fishing rod — half-
closing day in Africa.'

None of this stands up to a moment's inspection. Rocks are not
bright, interesting colours at all — they are always arts 'n' craft
hues, that is, brown, brown-grey, grey-grey, grey-brown and off-
yellow. They never look like their names — heaven help anyone
who goes in search of something that looks as if it should be called
lower greensands. And, worst of all, stones that look exactly the
same are, as usual, from different families, whereas pebbles that
you and I can see a mile off are totally unrelated always turn out to
be granites with different dyes or preservatives used in their
manufacture.

What you and I need is none of this. We need merely to learn what
is the main stone in the area we happen to be in. And luckily there is
a perfectly good method of finding out which no book on geology, as
far as I know, has ever been based on. *Go straight to the nearest church
and see what it is made of.*

Churches in the good old days were always built of the local
building material, so much so that I have decided to reclassify all
geological deposits as 'churchstone'. The advantages are obvious.
Churches are all above ground — no messy digging around to find

bits of rock. Churchstone has been cut and fitted by practised workmen — no chance of picking up the wrong thing by mistake. Churches are not confusing jig-saw puzzles unlike the ground you are standing on. Churchstone is geology with the heartache taken out of it.

So, if you are interested in the local geology, here's what to do.

1. Find a good solid-looking church or, even better, a tumble-down church.
2. Get out your hammer and chisel.
3. Chip off a decent sample.
4. Take it home with you.
5. Identify it.

A word of warning: cathedrals are useless for this. They have always been built from snobby imported stone, brought in large barges from across the Channel for the purpose. Chipping away at cathedrals, especially in the south of England, will tell you a great deal about geology in Normandy but that is not why you and I go nature-spotting — not me, at least.

And cathedrals are usually too well guarded, whereas little country churches are visited only by the occasional brass-rubber and flower-

arranger. If however you should be challenged by the vicar, show him this certificate. It should work like a shot.

From the Society for Entry
Into Rural Churches
To the Rev whomsoever it may concern,
                    Hi! Today I, the undersigned, attempted to visit your charming little church but found it firmly locked. I am now attempting to make a new entrance. I hope this meets with your approval.

love and peace

If you agree not to make a large hole in the East Wall, the vicar will generally let you keep a small piece of churchstone, relieved that nothing worse has happened.

Churchstone

The ten basic types.

COTSWOLD HONEYSTONE

Perhaps the nicest of all British churchstones. It is immediately identifiable from its soft yellow colour and from the cosy warm feeling it gives you, also from the foolish urge it gives you to say out loud: 'You know, the British countryside is still there if you know where to look for it', then look round, embarrassed.

One good test for Cotswold Honeystone churches is to frame your hands into a rectangle, then look at the church through it, trying to imagine that underneath the picture all the days in March are listed and that on top is printed 'With The Compliments of Geoff's Car Repair Service, Batheaston'. If it looks right, you are right. For this reason it is also sometimes known as Calendarstone.

As a final test, sniff it. It should smell faintly of afternoon teas.

LAGER AND LIMESTONE

A decent, unpretentious northern stone, normally browny-grey or gravy-brown or Brownie-green or Graham-Greene or any old colour. It is widely found in the north of England, also the south, where in some areas it has replaced the Great Northern Bitterstone, and vice versa. There is nothing very exciting about Lager and Limestone, but nothing unfriendly either.

Lager and Limestone was formed millions of years ago by gradual deposits of yeast, water, malt and dust. Occasionally it contains a fossilised slice of lemon.

SCOTS GREYSTONE

Occasionally known as granite. Most towns in Scotland are built out of this hard, grey, black, pink, durable, indestructible material. Any other stone would have been washed away by the rain long ago. When it is covered in soot, it does not change colour.

One can identify it immediately by the pictures it conjures up of dark, wet evenings in Scottish towns. Sniff it, and you can almost smell the far-away scent of fish and chips emanating from the one establishment that still stays open after 6 pm in the average Scottish town, mingling with the no less pungent odours of mealie pudding, deep-fried haggis and lightly fried *Glasgow Herald*.

Scotland, but not Wales, note. The stone of Wales is slate (see Flagstone). Scots Greystone was formed zillions of years ago in a tremendous upheaval, almost certainly on a Saturday night.

PINKSTONE

In some parts of Britain the local churchstone has a definite reddish tinge, for example Devon and Cheshire, as well as up the Avon where it is known locally as Double Gloucester. This is either because it was formed millions of years ago in a fiery upheaval or because it was made from deposits of little red sea creatures which formed a sedimentary layer on, etc. Either way, it is known to geologists as sandstone for the very good reason that geologists always name things after something they don't resemble. (Try getting what they call flint into a cigarette lighter, or writing with 'chalk' or making coffee mugs out of 'clay'. Better still, don't try. If you don't believe me, try washing your hands with 'soapstone'.)

It's a nice little stone, unpretentious, in colour somewhere between a gritty Rioja and a maroon jumper that needs washing badly.

EDDYSTONE

Some kinds of rock seem multi-coloured and have wavy patterns through them, as if they set out to be Plasticine and had a change of heart halfway through. This is because they were formed billions of years ago by deposits of sediment at the bottom of very stormy lakes, during thunder and lightning.

Eddystone, if you look at it closely, turns out to be softer in some parts than others, and these soft parts erode over the years, leaving only the hard bits behind. This means that any church built out of Eddystone will gradually get smaller through the centuries. There isn't much you can do about this, except to remember to stoop as you go in through the door.

FLINTSTONE

The only kind of churchstone which is not big enough to get decent blocks out of. It comes in small round dollops, which are usually stuck ornamentally on the towers of churches, the churches themselves being built out of chalk, plaster of Paris or one of those new wonder products which always go dry before you apply them.

In some parts of the country you may still find old folk playing the traditional game called flint-knapping, which is very like conkers but much more dangerous.

QUARTZSTONE

Any churchstone which tends in the least to sparkle, or at least to be made up of thousands of particles and look like petrified Perrier, is quartzstone. It makes an ideal churchstone, of course, as it provides a handy method of driving the church clock.

MILLS AND BOONSTONE

Sylvia shrank terrified against the church wall, and stared into the hungry eyes of Sebastian. Her thin summer dress felt no protection at all against his devouring gaze, and the handsome head she had once so admired seemed now only to leer at her.

'What do you want, Sebastian?' she said, holding her head up proudly. I mustn't let him see that I'm scared, she thought.

'You didn't think I brought you out here just to look at old churches, did you?' said Sebastian hoarsely, his voice thickened by desire. 'You silly little thing, don't you realise how much I've longed for you? And now, here, alone . . .'

Oh, Humphrey, thought Sylvia. You may be boring and a rotten dresser, but it's you I want, not this . . . this adventurer. She scrabbled at the old church wall behind her, as if hoping that a secret door would open up, and to her surprise a chunk of the old masonry came away in her hand. Without thinking, she swung it up and brought it down on Sebastian's head. He looked faintly surprised as he fell unconscious into the patch of briars and nettles behind him.

Yes, soft and crumbly Mills and Boonstone may not be much good as a churchstone, but it can be pretty helpful in a tight spot. It's not unlike Lymeswold, but much cheaper.

FLAGSTONE or GRAVESTONE

One of the things that made Sebastian look faintly surprised as he fell into the patch of weeds was that his head hit something pretty hard. It was a gravestone. These are always made out of gravestone, or what the Welsh call slate. It comes in great big slabs and is never used for building churches, only graves and roofs. (In Wales they tend to have chapels rather than churches, and to build them out of corrugated iron; with so few chapels now being built, the Welsh steel industry is in a bad way.)

This hard grey churchstone is very smooth and is the only kind of stone which it is easy to write on, hence the tendency among modern vicars to cover their gravestones in briars and nettles, to prevent graffiti appearing on them. How many caddish Casanovas like Sebastian lie mouldering and hidden on British graves, I hate to think.

GALLSTONE

A small, very hard growth of rock which individually can cause much pain and social distress, but which in large quantities (when it is known as gravel) is very useful for building modern churches. Gravel pits are easy to tell from other kinds of quarries as they are always full of water and covered with small sailing dinghies. Gravel is found almost exclusively on the edges of newer towns, and so are most modern churches; it is the world's only exclusively suburban rock.

A word of warning. There are many substances which seem from their name to be part of geology, but are not: e.g. Hailstone, Prunestone, Maidstone, Silverstone, Blackpool Rock, etc. Pumice Stone is not native to this country; if found, it is only a bathroom escape.

Another word of warning. Occasionally the reader will find him or herself in a part of the country where there are no churches — on Dartmoor, perhaps, in the Scottish Highlands or at Milton Keynes. I would move somewhere else if I were you.

Section Fourteen

Dead Things Lying On the Ground

Despite the fact that almost everything in nature becomes a dead thing lying on the ground sooner or later, this is not a subject that attracts many people. Things that move around and look cute on television are what interests people, which is why there are plenty of societies for the protection of birds, animals, etc, and no Royal Society for the Protection of Dead Things Lying on The Ground. This is human nature and there is nothing we can do about it. I will therefore keep this section mercifully brief.

FOSSILS

Any plant or animal which has taken longer than a million years to rot down into humus can be called a fossil. As it has meanwhile turned into stone, it probably never will rot down.

N.B. I know that it doesn't really turn into stone — the stone merely bears the imprint of the vanished creature. But, as I said, I am trying to keep this section brief.

NUTS

A nut is a fruit which breaks your teeth. Nature has devised some wonderful ways of spreading its seed, and encasing it in a hard shell which has to be broken open with a hammer is not one of them. Most human tools are unable to open a brazil nut; how is an animal expected to cope? How do brazil trees ever have a family?

Another major difference between nuts and fruit is that a fruit looks the same on the tree or the ground as it does on a market stall; a nut never does. Who would think that a walnut in the wild is soft and green, or that brazil nuts come packed a dozen at a time in large wooden fruits weighing 4 lbs? The first time I ever saw a cashew tree I got the shock of my life; the cashew nut grows hanging from a large pear.

You might recognise peanuts on the tree. Except that they don't grow where you can see them, but underground. By growing seeds underground nature seems to have got it right for once.

My advice: don't be a nut-spotter.

PERMAMUD

The British equivalent of permafrost, which covers vast areas of Siberia and never thaws. Permamud is mud which never dries; it is found at the entrance to cow fields, under bright green grass on hillsides, between the river and the bank, at the edge of lanes where you want to park your car, round back doors, on playing fields and throughout the house after country walks. It is rich in fibre and roughage. Worms love it. Nobody else does.

FLINTS

Small flints are found on the ground throughout Britain. This is because the screw at the bottom of the cigarette lighter has worked loose. Once you have found the flint, you must find the screw and spring as well. Then you must try to get them all back in. Then you must go and buy a box of matches.

COWPATS

You will need a box of matches to test cowpats with. Traditionally, dried animal dung is used as fuel throughout the Third World, but try as I may, I have never succeeded in setting fire to a cowpat, however dried and desiccated. It is your turn to have a go.

PEVSNERITE

Nikolaus Pevsner is the brave man who set out to describe all the outstanding buildings in England in a succession of county-by-county volumes, though in many places he seems to have limited himself to the local church or manor house — in other words, places locked against you and me. Encouraged by his interest, many buildings have been given preservation orders by the athorities; sadly, this is often the prelude to their being burnt or pulled down the next day. All that remains is a pile of curiously-carved building material.

This is known to scientists as pevsnerite.

CHARCOAL

At the end of the Middle Ages many forests were chopped down to provide fuel to make charcoal, which was in great demand for the Renaissance fashion of drawing in black and white. In some parts of Britain you can still find deposits of charcoal left behind when oil painting came into fashion. Now photography is all the rage, and we have an oil glut. So it goes.

OLD SKINS

As you must have seen on television, some classes of animal, snake and insect slough off their old skins and grow new ones. They just leave the old ones lying around. This is nature's equivalent of discarded jeans or worn-out gloves.

HUMUS

Everything in nature, apart from geology, rots down sooner or later to make a kind of rich brown wholefood on which the rest of nature feeds. This is known as humus, though it is sometimes called after its discoverer, John Innes; it is very important to leave it where it is and not disturb the ecology. The Greeks have attempted to popularise humus as an hors d'oeuvre, which probably explains why so much of Greece is bare and arid.

DROPPINGS

This is not a prudish book, so it has to be mentioned somewhere that, when not breeding and eating, nature spends most of its time going to the lavatory. Except that it hasn't any lavatories. So many of the things you find on the ground are exactly what they look like, though they will have different names depending on the source of the dropping — sheep's flung, rabbit sporran, cow dripping, horsefruit, beefpats, etc.

It all rots down nicely, so the system seems quite admirable. Man is the only creature that seems to have the time and energy to pump all his sewage out to sea, and then go swimming in it. Man is also the only creature who can be bothered to pick up other animals' droppings and put them in sacks in order to drop them on the ground again. Not just animals, either. Trees, as well. What are leaves if not tree droppings? What are compost heaps if not piles of manure?

I have nothing against this. I just wonder sometimes what trees think to themselves when they see mankind come along and put their droppings into sacks. However, an examination of tree psychology is beyond the scope of this book.

N.B. Anything in Section Eighteen, Dead Things That Can Fly Faster Than You Can Run, can be mistaken for anything in this chapter as soon as it has landed.

Section Fifteen

Dead Things Lying On the Beach

The area between the high-tide and low-tide marks on a beach is known as the foreshore. Twice a day the sea advances from one to the other, then goes back, making the foreshore the only part of nature which is provided with regular cleaning arrangements. The size of the foreshore depends very much on its angle of slope; in Morecambe Bay the sea seems to go in and out several miles a day, whereas at the foot of cliffs the tide doesn't even go in and out, just up and down a few feet. In the Mediterranean, where tides are virtually unknown, the foreshore is considered very big if it is more than two inches.

This explains, incidentally, why you won't find the word 'foreshore' in English-Italian dictionaries. They haven't got one and don't need a word for it. The concept, with which we are so familiar, of holidaymakers being cut off by the advancing tide, would make no sense at all to an Italian. If a holidaymaker can't sprint two inches, I think he'd say, then he has no business being on the beach in the first place.

It may even be true that all those holidaymakers in Britain that we read about being cut off from the mainland by the tide are Italian visitors, totally amazed to find that the sea has moved round behind them while they were polishing off the salami and mozzarella salad. I hasten to add that I have no evidence for this, I just find it a pleasing theory. However, speculation on the racial origin of travellers cut off by our tides is beyond the scope of this book, indeed beyond the scope of any book I can think of.*

91

*Though there may be some useful information in the lyrics of Acker Bilk's tune, 'Stranger on the Shore'. If it has any lyrics.

Where were we? Oh, yes. The foreshore, then, is cleaned every day. But unfortunately the very same tides which wash and brush up the shore also deposit an immense amount of rubbish on it. Anything the sea doesn't want, it dumps on our beaches. And anything which dies out to sea, and is too light to sink to the sea bottom, floats to its final resting place on the foreshore. (It must be a very crowded two inches round the Mediterranean, though this too is beyond the scope of this book.)

This explains why nothing lives on the foreshore. Anything that does try living on the foreshore finds it has to move out twice a day to avoid drowning, and when it comes back after high tide discovers that its little patch of land is full of new rubbish left by the sea. Or panic-stricken Italians, of course. Either way, it's no place to live and it soon gives up, going off to make its home under beach chalets or in the town sewage system.

It might be said that a very few forms of life do brave it out on the foreshore by going into a permanent coma, like limpets. But it's not what I call living.

BURNT OUT STARFISH

Astronomers tell us that even the brightest and biggest star will eventually die, either burning out or exploding spectacularly and leaving behind a black hole into which, if I've got it straight, even the biggest telescope will one day be sucked, and starfish are much the same. Burning furiously, they plunge into the sea at night and are immediately extinguished, to be washed up the next morning; a good fall of blazing starfishes is something which, once seen, is not likely to be forgotten.

I personally do not believe that starfish ever implode to become black holes, but many marine biologists hope that, by studying the bodies of now-extinct starfish, we can one day discover how the sea started — with a big splash, as some believe, or through gradual seepage or simply by God saying: Let there be water, buckets, spades, etc.

COLD SPIRALS

On the sand near the edge of the water you will often find small, intricately-woven spiral patterns which look like spaghetti till you find they are made of sand. Are they, as the experts think, left behind by worms living beneath the surface of the sand? Are they made by artistically-minded cuttlefish? Do they indicate a tendency of the earth to sweat through its pores?

In preference to these implausible theories, I prefer to believe that this spaghetti-like stuff really is spaghetti, left behind and decomposed. But who would leave it behind? Italian holiday-makers, of course, stranded by the tide in the middle of their pasta picnic.

LEFT-OVER JELLYFISH

You sometimes come across on the beach soft shapeless blobs of jelly, for all the world like unwanted dessert or pudding that the sea felt too full for and simply threw away like scraps off a plate. In fact, scientists now think this is exactly what they are, and that the sea somehow has an appetite which can get sated. People who live by the sea often talk about things being 'thrown up' on the beach. Scientists now think this is exactly what happens. They don't say it out loud, but that's what they think. They are now working on the theory that storms at sea are some form of indigestion.

LIMPETS EN SAISON

Any shellfish which clings to a rock in a permanent coma is a limpet. Limpet-watching is one of the less active areas of nature study and is not recommended to most readers; during a prolonged bout of limpet-watching the tide may creep round you unnoticed, especially if you come from a part of the world where there are no tides. The only proven way of removing a limpet from a rock is with a small controlled explosive device, often known as a limpet mine. This usually removes the rock as well.

SEAFOOD SHELLS

Shellfish are much more commonly found without the fish inside. There are many different shapes, pleasingly patterned with attractive colours, such as you might find piled up on a table after some full and satisfying meal set up by an Italian family. Many scientists now believe that this is exactly what they are. The only thing that puzzles them is what happened to the Italian family.

DISUSED DETECTORS

The main industry in Cornwall for many years was waiting for ships to get wrecked; traditionally you could then go aboard and fight the sailors for the cargo. The modern equivalent of this is treasure-seeking, and you can often see keen young collectors out with metal detectors looking for treasure trove, and fighting people from national museums for their finds.

Nowadays almost all the things worth finding (Italian jewellery, small lira coins, priceless reproduction Renaissance art from Italy) have been found, and most collectors give up and go home. The most you are likely to find is detectors thrown away in disgust.

FROTH

The yellow foam found at the edge of the sea on a windy day is a familiar sight to all of us. Who has not felt strangely moved at the sight of the salty spume blown off the sea, lying rich and golden at our feet? And which one of us has paused to wonder how on earth a white powder like salt could possibly turn into a *yellow froth*?

Scientists are now inclined to think it is probably zabaglione.

LUMPS OF CONCRETE

It is odd how often we find large blocks of concrete on the foreshore. We find many other kinds of man-made refuse, of course, notably polystyrene beakers and crisp packets, but these are easily washed in from nearby oil rigs. It is less easy to imagine concrete bobbing in on a wave.

Much research has been done on this in Sicily. Local scientists have stationed observers with concrete lumps by the water's edge — indeed, they have stationed observers *in* concrete lumps by the water's edge — to see if the incoming tide would wash them away. The tidal movement of two inches has not proved enough to verify the theory or disprove it.

Scientists now think that these Sicilian experiments may have been transferred to British shores, where the tides are good and reliable; hence the presence of so much concrete. The only thing that puzzles them is what happened to the observers.

NON-RETURNABLE BOTTLES

A non-returnable bottle may be defined as one which, if you throw it from the beach into the sea, does not come back. What it does do is float out to sea and then, by some homing instinct which we do not yet fully understand, travel round the Bay of Biscay, pass through the Straits of Gibraltar and end up on the shores of Italy. Here it mates with the local Chianti or Orvieto Secco bottles, and its offspring eventually make the arduous journey back to our shores and arrive fully grown in time for the next summer season. Here it simply waits on the beach until some kind passer-by throws it back into the sea to start the long journey back again.

We are often disappointed to find the bottles contain no message, but the reason for this is quite simple; most people throw bottles out to sea without bothering to put messages in them. They are nature's equivalent of unsolicited mail.

Some kinds of Italian bottle, incidentally, grow a straw wrapping which goes water-logged and sinks immediately. If you should find one on an English beach, it has not floated all the way from Italy; it has been left behind by an Italian family recently cut off by the tide. There may be a message inside. It probably says something like: 'Hey! Whatsa going on here? Is England sinking? Or is the sea overflowing? We want our money back!'

More rarely, you will find bottles containing miniature ships, or even a good helping of Chianti. Rarest of all, a bottle with light bulb, flex and lampshade adorned with Italian wine labels.

DEAD LETTERS

The amazing journeys of eels to the Sargasso Sea and back again is as nothing compared to the life story of letters found tossing around on the sea-shore. These have started life as mighty trees in the Canadian forests, been turned into pulp by man, and converted into paper by other men. Then, by some homing instinct which we do not fully understand, they congregate on shelves in W H Smith's in Guildford, before being turned into letters from Aunty Mabel and abandoned on the beach by Aunty Mabel's relatives, or by postmen with too much mail to deliver.

Very rarely you may find letters which have started life on the beach. In Italian, they read something like: 'Well, Roberto, this looks like curtains. The piece of beach where we are having our English picnic is floating out to sea, and I am writing to say goodbye. I wish I had listened to you when you say, English holidays are bad news. I met a lovely boy in the disco last night at Clinton-on-Sea, but now I will never see him again. Well, that is all my news, so I will say goodbye from Lucia. PS, also goodbye from Silvia, Pietro, Francesca, the twins, Aunt Bella, Lodovico, Alfredo . . .'

The letter usually tails off about there.

N.B. I have not bothered to describe the many stones you will find on the average English bathing beach, as they are not on the beach so much as part of it. Stones are sand which has not been ground down yet. Scientists now think that stones are part of the sea's digestive system and form an important element of roughage.

Section Sixteen

Dead Things Stuck in the Ground

Most of these are not natural at all, but man-made. However, they should be mentioned somewhere in this book, as they form the basis of two sciences which have grown immensely popular recently. These are:—

Industrial Archaeology, which believes that a thing that doesn't work any more is far more interesting than a thing that still works. This has almost completely replaced industry itself in some parts of Britain.

Ancientology, which believes that Britain is joined by a mysterious set of invisible lines and that if we could only crack the secret we could all be ancient Britons again. What the advantage of this would be, ancientologists do not say.

TRIANGULATION POINTS

Small pyramids of stone, usually marked on Ordnance Survey maps, which have brass plaques with mysterious numbers inscribed on them. Legend has it that some ancient British tribe used them to get from place to place. However, these pyramids are always found on lonely hilltops with the dark coming down and the rain sweeping in, the nearest pub five miles away and closing time approaching, so the tribe presumably did not last long or, if it did, was pretty miserable.

97

These triangulation points are now of great help to the Ordnance Survey; in some strange way it helps them to raise the price of maps every month.

OBELISKS

Huge pyramids of stone, usually placed on top of hills or at awkward bends in the road. Ancientologists claim that Britain is linked by invisible lines starting with the Scott Monument in Edinburgh, going down to Cleopatra's Needle in London, and formed by all these obelisks. The theory is that they were all built by an eighteenth- and nineteenth-century tribe who worshipped the remains of departed authors and army generals, especially if they had fallen in battle in India.

PYLONS

The theory is that these huge metal masts link Britain by a series of visible lines carrying funny stuff called electricity which makes people's toasters and juke boxes work. Everybody believes this except ancientologists, who think it is too fantastical for words.

HUGE HOLES IN HILLS

There are so many holes in hills in Britain that a book could be written about them. In fact, I am amazed that nobody has yet written a book about them, as books have been written about everything else. To be quite honest, I expect the publication of this book, if it does nothing else, to produce a flood of angry letters: 'Dear Mr Kington, How could you remain in ignorance of my definitive work *Britain's Ancient Holes* (Strangestuff Press, 1977, £60) which proves that a series of mysterious underground lines . . .?'

Among the major causes of British hill holes are, with number of sightings, old Roman mines (3,480), railway ventilation shafts (540), quarries for obelisk stone (980), Luftwaffe raids on hills lit up to look like Liverpool (325) and abortive TV digs in the side of Silbury Hill (4).

STANDPIPES

These mysterious objects are simply wooden posts with metal pipes attached. Industrial archaeologists claim that they date from early 1983, when a water-workers' strike made necessary the emergency supply of water. If this is so, they argue, they should be preserved as a unique example of a time when this wettest of all islands went short of water.

Ancientologists do not yet claim that standpipes form a sacred series of lines throughout Britain, but these are early days.

TV MASTS

These are immensely high and thin posts, which are built to support red lights, which are supposed to warn aeroplanes of the presence of the thin and high posts. Their secondary use is to link the country in a series of invisible lines which will enable people to watch documentary programmes about ancientology or industrial archaeology. This is known as BBC-2. They occur only on top of high lonely hills.

(Somewhere there must be a high hill-top with a triangulation point, obelisk, TV mast and stand-pipe, all dangerously close to a railway ventilation shaft, with a plaque saying proudly: 'European Museum of the Year 1979.')

DUTCH ELM DISEASE TREES

It is sometimes said that the elm has almost totally disappeared from our landscape. This is rubbish; it's still there, but dead. Farmers are legally meant to chop diseased elms down but as there's no money in it for them, or threat from the trees to their livelihood, nothing happens. As a result, the British landscape is dotted with corpses.

If dead elms did disappear, two things would happen. There would be a theory that Britain used to be joined by a series of lines between elm trees, and there would be a clamour for the last few to be preserved as a historical monument.

PILES OF ROCK

These are never just piles of rock — they are cairns, or ruined bothies, or old butt and bens, or industrial remains. If the ancientologists get there first, they will be pieced together again into Celtic dwellings; an industrial archaeologist would prefer to reassemble them as a smelter's cottage. What they really are, of course, is just piles of rock.

PILES OF ROCK WITH WINDOW-HOLES IN

These are the heart and soul of industrial archaeology, because they used to be water mills, wind mills, coffee mills, pepper mills, dark satanic mills of all kinds, dating back to a day when Britain was joined by a mysterious line of treacherous, muddy, almost impassable main roads. They will all one day be restored to non-working condition and reopened to the public.

Ancientologists, who generally have absolutely no interest in industry of any kind, except publishing, ignore these structures completely. Except in Wales, curiously enough, where they claim they are burnt-out cottages belonging to the English, and used by a tribe called the Welsh Liberation Army as the centre of a mysterious web of lines which lead to a Welsh-speaking and completely independent Wales. Scientists now believe that Stonehenge may once have been a large Saxon weekend cottage in Welsh territory.

WEATHER POSTS

Sometimes, on exposed uplands, you will find posts stuck in the ground beside the road. They are there so that when the ground is blanketed by snow you will know, from the posts, where the road is.

At the approach to fords or low bridges you will sometimes find posts with numbers painted on, to indicate the height of the flooding that sometimes covers the lower part of the posts.

In rivers you will often see posts or withies stuck to indicate where the navigable channel meets the dangerous shallows on either side.

All of these are tremendously useful, so neither ancientologists nor industrial archaeologists have ever shown the slightest interest in them.

Section Seventeen

Jetsam, Flotsam, Etcsam

This section is slightly harder to justify in a nature guide — even one as unusually comprehensive as this one — because things floating in water are usually man-made, or at least man-dropped, and therefore not exactly part of nature. On the other hand, they also tend to change their identity in the water, usually in the first five minutes, and in their new water-logged, bloated or discoloured state might be taken for part of nature, if this chapter was not here to alert you.

I have also decided that it was high time the concept of flotsam and jetsam was updated. This rough-and-ready description may have been all right in the days of clippers and schooners, when almost everything was biodegradable or at least useful, but we are now in a much more sophisticated age of litter. Just to remind you . . .

Jetsam is stuff deliberately thrown overboard, usually to lighten a ship. This obviously includes such things as oil slicks, tins which have gone past the sell-by date and stowaways.

Flotsam is stuff which has simply fallen off a ship, such as plastic mugs, containers full of cars and drunken Greek captains.

Well, this distinction seems far too broad to be of much use. I have in fact found a third word in my travels which is 'lagan' and means 'goods or refuse to be found on the sea bed', but this is rarely useful in everyday conversation because most of us do not go exploring on the seabed or, if we do, try not to drag it into our everyday conversation. (An exception must be made for Prince Charles and the *Mary Rose*.)

So what I propose is to throw jetsam, flotsam and lagan overboard for ever and to equip ourselves with the following ten useful bits of rubbish.

DROPSAM

Stuff that has been dropped overboard by accident, leading to an abject apology to the skipper. Things that people really wanted to keep but which, well, just slipped through their fingers and they're terribly sorry. This includes corkscrews, full bottles of alcohol, corks from half-full bottles of alcohol, charts, newspapers, stamps about to be put on postcards, postcards which had just had stamps put on them, copies of this book, ropes, fenders, yachting caps and the last box of matches on board.

PLANKSAM

People who have just been dropped overboard for losing dropsam.

NETSAM

Things dropped accidentally from the riverbank by an angler. More rarely, the remains of a contest between angler and fish, which the fish has won.

JEANSAM

Articles of clothing which have disappeared overboard while the owner was changing from one set of clothes to another.

BITSAM

Small objects without which something else on the boat will not work.

WRECKSAM

Things on a boat which will not work, due to bitsam, and which have just been thrown overboard in a blind rage. (Not to be confused with the Welsh town of the same name but different spelling.)

WEEDSAM

Great clumps of weed which have uprooted themselves and are floating downstream in a praiseworthy attempt to find a better neighbourhood.

DRINKSAM

Any disposable object pertaining to the beverage industry. There are over 500,000 known species of this family, of which the most common tend to be beer mats, plastic or polystyrene mugs, lids, plastic spoons, sachets of sugar, cuppa soup packets, swizzle-sticks, coloured straws, maraschino cherries, beer cans and champagne corks. Quite frankly, this is the sort of thing which conferences on Sea Law should be worrying about, not oil in the Antarctic and the plight of penguins. Anyone who has ever seen a plastic mug slick will not forget it easily.

DRIFTSAM

Totally valueless pieces of pebble, wood, glass, etc, which are found on the sea shore and then polished and carved by people who have just moved out of London until they can be sold for large amounts of money in craft shops.

ETCSAM

Anything else. Also, driftsam which has failed to reach its price, or any price, and has been thrown back on the sea shore.

Section Eighteen

*Dead Things That Can Fly Faster Than
You Can Run*

This is a new section that has never appeared in any nature guide
before. It is designed to be used after the following conversation has
taken place.

'Oh, look — what's that?'

'You mean, the thing flying over the nettles and into the
brambles?'

'Yes. Go and get it.'

'No.'

'I wonder what it was.'

It was one of the following.

LONG, THIN, WHITE FLYING THING

Sometimes known as gossamer. Spiders are the SAS of nature, and
will spend hours flying through the air on their ropes, prior to
landing and subjecting some hapless insect to savage interrogation.
The question they usually ask is: 'Have you any last requests?'

LITTLE, WHITE, PARACHUTE THINGS

The ability of dandelions to tell the time is somewhat exaggerated, owing to the fact that there is always one seed that refuses to be blown off; the time usually turns out to be 37 o'clock. Nevertheless people go on trying, which explains the presence of these little, white parachute things. Don't forget — in October, dandelions have to go back one hour.

SMALL, WHIRLING HELICOPTER THINGS

The helicopter was invented, not by Leonardo da Vinci, but by the lime tree. It is used in nature to spread the seeds as far as possible: in human terms, the urge of the parent to get rid of the children as soon as possible. The basic urge of the lime tree is to cover the entire surface of the earth with lime trees, which would mean of course that you couldn't park your car anywhere without it getting covered in sticky stuff. I think we can afford to be ruthless to helicopter seeds and shoot them down as they pass.

SMALL, WHIRLING WHITE SHREDS

These are pieces of airline napkin. They have fallen from an aeroplane above. This can only happen if the aeroplane has blown up. Run for your life.

SMALL, WHIRLING WHITE DOTS

These are called snowflakes. One of the miracles of nature is that under the microscope all snowflakes look different. The miracle is not that they look different — it is that anyone has managed to get them under a microscope. Can you imagine sitting in the snow with a microscope, pushing these little things under before they melt? Personally, I don't think it's possible. I think all those snowflakes in photographs have been made in the laboratory, or chipped off out-of-control deep freezes.

108

LONG, CURLY, COLOURED THINGS

These are parts of a bird called feathers. Birds use them for warmth, for flying, for letting water run off and, in the old days, for writing long letters with. When they are worn out, birds simply drop them in flight. Human beings tend to pick them up and keep them, to stuff into duvets. Birds, on the other hand, like to pick up human hair when it has been discarded and turn it into *their* bedding. This is one of ecology's little jokes.

SMALL, DARK THINGS TRAVELLING AT OVER 300 MPH

When bits of other planets enter our atmosphere they start to burn up, and by the time they land, they are just the right size to put in the local museum on a piece of card reading: 'Found locally; origin unknown.' Don't try to catch them. You'd look silly with a hole through your hand.

SMALL, DARK THINGS TRAVELLING AT UNDER 300 MPH

When bits of our trees enter our atmosphere, they start to dodge round all over the place and it is impossible to catch them. One can spend a happy afternoon trying to grab leaves as they fall, as long as you don't mind the mounting frustration. Once they land, they become part of nature's droppings. (See *Moulds.*)

SMALL, DARK THINGS GOING UPWARDS

Bits from a nearby bonfire.

SMALL, SHINY FRAGMENTS MARKED 'MADE IN USA' OR 'MADE IN USSR'.

Bits of a nearby satellite.

Section Nineteen

Things Flying Way Out Of Reach, or Basic Clouds

Meteorology is an unfortunate science. For one thing, it should be, but isn't, the study of meteors. For another thing, it has been on the retreat for the last thirty years, unlike most sciences.

In the 1950s it was thought that we were on the verge of being able to control the weather. Cloud-seeding was the coming thing, a process of sowing clouds with small particles to make them rain, rather as film stars can be made artificially to cry. Experiments have now been going on for thirty years, till it was announced very quietly in 1982 that the programme was to be called off: in all that time only one rain shower had been caused, and that not very impressive.

Meanwhile, if control was not possible, at least we thought we could push ahead with forecasting. Satellite photography in the 1970s gave rise to the long-range weather forecast, a month at a time. This in turn gave rise to the observation that the long-range weather forecast was wrong most of the time. In turn, this gave rise to the dropping of the long-range weather forecast, and to the admission that really accurate forecasting could only cover the next day or two, and not always then.

In other words, we are now back roughly to where we were in the 1950s, with added distrust. The only real advance that has been achieved is the creation of prettier weather maps on TV and friendlier weathermen. It isn't a great deal to show for thirty years' progress. Perhaps they would have been better off studying meteors.

I suspect also that meteorology has been retarded by the strict adherence to Latin names for clouds. Other naturalists are more tolerant about this and will unbend enough to talk about the oak, toad and buttercup instead of insisting on quercus, bufo bufo and ranunculus. But meteorologists will never admit that there is an English word for cumulus or cirrus. We're quite lucky, all things considered, that they don't insist on *fronto calidus aut frigidus* for warm or cold front. Still, meteorologists have more to hide than other people, so I suppose we must forgive them for using Latin for the purpose.

Here, rendered into English at last, are the ten main kinds of cloud, and what they mean.

STOCKING MASK CLOUDS

When bank robbers put on their face disguises, or young children pull mummy's tights over their head and frighten her out of her life, their faces are quite hideously distorted and threatening. There is a certain kind of cloud like this; as soon as it passes in front of the sun, the sun leers at you like a child-molester or a Vatman through the dirty fabric racing across it. This cloud brings rain. Also hail, snow, sleet, frogs, locusts, lightning, thunder and blood on the moon.

MACKEREL CLOUDS

Mackerel clouds should be bright and shiny, plump with glistening sides. If they are dull and grey, have nothing to do with them. It will only rain.

COTTON WOOL CLOUD

This is the familiar cloud you get on a typical English summer day, looking so pretty and white against the blue sky. Confusingly, it also occurs on a typical freezing English winter day, but in either case it is what is known as a fair weather cloud — that is, it will almost certainly rain in an hour or two. The main consolation is that those cotton wool clouds will be back again soon after that.

Don't forget that at dusk these pretty white clouds look dark and threatening. Otherwise they are just the same.

HIGH FLYING FEATHERS

On a typical summer day, and also on a typical winter day — this applies to spring and autumn as well — you often get very high wispy white clouds at, I don't know, maybe 20,000 feet, or 30,000 feet, maybe even 50,000 feet. If you see these, it is a sure sign that there is nothing in between you and them, which to that extent is a good sign. On the other hand, they are what is known as clouds of change, which means that very soon you can expect change.

In other words, rain.

These feathery clouds are so high that they are, in fact, particles of ice. What this means is that if you fly through them in a plane, you'll be deafened by the noise on the windscreen.

GREAT GREY GREEN GREASY CLOUDS

These clouds are the colour of washing-up water. They come in over the rooftops at great speed, with the texture of torn up J cloths. Occasionally they part to reveal a plane looking desperately for Heathrow, like a forgotten spoon at the bottom of the kitchen sink. Then they close up again, like washing-up water coming over the top of the sink, too deep to put your hand in to grab the plug. Still, at least they don't presage rain.

This is because it's raining already.

Soon they will pass over and the sun will come out to light up the landscape, glinting and gleaming like crockery you forgot to rinse the Fairy Green Liquid off.

FAIRY GREEN LIQUID CLOUDS

These usually occur towards sunset, when the setting sun lights up the bank of clouds on the horizon with all the colours of the spectrum — orange, lemon, lime, raspberry, violet, elizabeth, bott. They make the perfect end to a perfect day, and Turner himself would not be ashamed of the melodramatic effects.

Shortly afterwards, it will come on to rain.

CAMERA CLUB CLOUDS

These are the clouds beloved of amateur photographers. Go into any exhibition by the local camera club and I will guarantee that the pictures that do not contain animals, girlfriends or flowers will feature dramatic banks of clouds, back-lit, the sun bursting through, shafts of light going mad, a hint of thunder, Beethoven's Pastoral Symphony written all over them. Occasionally they occur at night, with the moon playing the part of the sun, who is temporarily indisposed, thank you.

They are direct descendants of the clouds featured in grand old oil paintings, what you might call classical cherub clouds, as in those days they all had little angels bursting from every nook and cranny, blowing trumpets and looking coy, with maybe St Agnes making a guest appearance or Joseph of Arimathea belting across at 20,000 feet. They often occur on ceilings. I am willing to wager that if 300 years ago you popped into an exhibition at Siena called 'Local Painting Club — Some Recent Ceilings', there would be nothing to see except classical cherub clouds. And animals, girlfriends and flowers of course.

They also occur in nature, but we tend not to notice them. We are too busy getting the umbrella up.

WORDSWORTH CLOUDS

This is the cloud that the poet wandered lonely as. No wonder the poet noticed it; clouds are normally very gregarious, and any lone cloud in an otherwise clear sky has got some explaining to do. Very probably it has just got cut off from the main herd or has lost its mother, but occasionally it is a rogue cloud looking for someone to rain on. I must say, if I looked down and saw an old poet mooning over some daffodils, I'd be very tempted.

EXPANDING STRING CLOUDS

When a plane flies very high overhead it often leaves behind a thin white line which gradually spreads to form something like tractor trails right across the sky. You can point to it and say smugly: 'It's not a cloud at all of course; it's just a vapour trail left by a plane.'

You'd be quite wrong. Anything that forms like a cloud *is* a cloud. Half the confusion in nature is caused by giving things different names, like saying that a cloud is a cloud in the sky but mist if it goes down the M1, and fog if it smells of industry. I sometimes wonder if this book hasn't come far too late.

Still, one thing you can say for the expanding string cloud. It doesn't bring rain.

BASIC JOHN INNES NO 1 CLOUD

This is the cloud you see when the sky can't be bothered to make any particular shape; it is just spread across the heavens in a uniform grey, peaty-brown sort of mixture, smoothed down at the edges to make sure there are no gaps at the horizon. Although nothing much to look at, it is very fertile, and within hours you should spot big fat drops of rain emerging from it.

Your Fellow Country-Lovers
or
Human Ecology In The Landscape

The average piece of British countryside looks, at first sight, quite empty of human beings. You might be forgiven for thinking that nobody lived there at all.

This is, in fact, very nearly true. Hardly anyone lives in the country any more. Some stockbrokers sleep there at night. Some farm workers come out very early to switch the machines on and come back late to switch them off again. There are occasional sightings of the near-extinct aristocracy, who live like Red Indians on their shrinking reservations, and dress not unlike them too. But it is so difficult actually to live in the country now that you are more likely to come across, in a ditch, the body of some poor person who decided to wait for a country bus until it arrived.

But wait for a while, keep very still, and they will start to arrive. Not country-dwellers, but people from the town who come out into the country for reasons of their own. Scientists are now beginning to think that there is a strange process going on whereby nature is going into the city and town-dwellers are being driven into the country. Hawks, buzzards, kestrels, foxes — all are being forced out of the country by chemicals and pesticides, while pollution, stress and pretty pictures on TV are tempting people out into the country, if only for the day.

117

These human visitors to the country are bound together by a fascinating chain of ecology, each one a link in the vital process that keeps the countryside from being totally depopulated. You, with your copy of *Nature Made Ridiculously Simple,* are just one of them, and it may be of interest to you to see how you fit in.

One of the rarest and most exotic visitors to the country is the *Fashion Model,* a pretty but apparently frail and helpless creature who flutters from pose to pose as if each one were her last. Desperately thin, she looks as if she could not even bear children to perpetuate her species. Fear not; in ten years' time she will be the fierce mother of five. Meanwhile, her delicate appearance masks an iron constitution which will get her through her task, whether it is to model tough country coats against the hard-wearing Cotswold Hills, or show off the slimmest of swimsuits in sub-zero Somerset.

The man who has brought her here is the *Fashion Photographer,* whose tough, masculine exterior masks a sensitive, shrinking nature. Dress him like the fashion model and he would die; he needs a

beard, tough leather clothes and liberal injections from a hip flask. He is a younger relative of . . .

The *Country Artist*, always an elderly man or woman who sits motionless in front of a canvas on which is depicted half a church. This they painted before you arrived and they will paint the rest after you've gone; while you're there, they remain absolutely motionless, because they can't stand being watched over their shoulder by

. . . *You.* You, I'm afraid, and me too, I'm afraid, are part of the large family of *Ramblers*. We are at the very low end of the scale, because we do not know where we are going, we turn aside at the slightest fancy and we never know quite enough about anything we are looking at. But at the top end of the scale comes the rambler proper, who does anything but ramble. Dressed in sensible, thick, green clothes, he marches across country armed with fiercely detailed maps, boots which would be the envy of the Falklands Task Force and copies of bye-laws covering every occasion. The only time he or she (the sex of the species is almost indistinguishable) shows any pleasure is when they discover a right of way which has been allowed to grow over, and which they can then trample through with a clear conscience, and a slight smile.

If anyone shows less evidence of pleasure than the rambler, it is the *Lone Bird-Watcher,* a near relative. Even when bird-watchers move in groups, they are still essentially lone. They never show pleasure, only dedication. Carrying quantities of telescopes, microphones, recorders and bird encyclopaedias, they move slowly, thoughtfully and unhappily into the most squashed, moist and inaccessible part of the country they can find, then remain there motionless. Birds flock from all over Europe to see this strange sight. The bird-watchers look at them. The birds look at the bird-watchers, who stare back. This stalemate might go on for months, if the birds did not vanish with the occasional thunderous arrival of . . .

. . . the *Police Cordon*. This is a collection of policemen in dull blue plumage, about eighty of them, side by side, walking across the landscape. Outlined on the skyline, or crashing through woods, they are hoping to remain invisible and inaudible until they can capture the . . .

. . . *Refugee From Justice*. This poor man has recently killed his wife or escaped from an unpleasant prison. Not unnaturally, he wants to put this part of his life behind him, but the police show no understanding of his problems and seem determined to rake up the past. In books the refugee would stumble into a farmhouse at the end of his tether and be hidden by a sympathetic farmer's wife, and then be handed over by the farmer who was in the pay of the villain. In real life, however, he simply gets away. The police would be better occupied, in my opinion, dealing with . . .

. . . the *Bluebell-Snatcher*, a townsman whose love of the country is expressed by taking as many armfuls of common flowers as he can

find. (If he takes very rare flowers, he is called something different: a botanist.) In winter, when there are no flowers, he takes young Christmas trees instead. You'd think that he would be a constant source of annoyance to . . .

. . . the *Farmer*, but you would be wrong. It is not generally understood that farmers hate nature and are glad to be rid of it. Just as the seaman hates and fears the sea, farmers loathe anything that threatens the one crop they are growing — to safeguard it, they are prepared to gas, bomb, dynamite, shoot, exterminate or wage chemical warfare on anything else. It is very rare to find a farmer who even likes gardening. Why should he spring to the defence of a bunch of bluebells?

No, all a farmer is interested in is making money, quite rightly, which is why the only person he respects is the *Egon Ronay Food Inspector*. He knows that in recent years Mr Ronay has lambasted motorway service areas, mainline station buffets and London tourist attraction cafeterias. He feels in his bones that it may be the turn of farmhouse teas next, so he turns his fearful eyes to any stranger coming up the farm track, for he does not know what an Egon Ronay food inspector looks like, and nor do we. Nor does he know that Egon Ronay's man is not looking at farms; he is at the local pub, waxing ecstatic over the fine wines, champagnes and sherries being handed out on silver salvers . . .

. . . to the *Hunters*, the only people you will see at pubs drinking on horseback. Just one quick drink they take, well, perhaps just one more large one, then, then off they gallop preceded by their hounds to track down and destroy their natural enemy, the *Saboteur*. This poor, harmless creature, dressed in anorak, NHS specs and gym shoes, utters constant wails of distress and outrage, but scientists now believe he may actually enjoy the chase. He makes his escape in small foreign cars or, more cunningly on a bicycle, though he should not be confused with . . .

. . . the bicyclist proper, who is always known as a *Cyclist*. His great joy in life is finding unspoilt spots of country where he can take photographs of his bicycle (large, foreground) in the landscape (out of focus, small grey background) which he will then send to magazines called *Touring Club Monthly* or *Wheeler*. He is dressed from head to foot in plastic trousers and has the amazing ability to wrap up all his worldly belongings in a thing the size of a tobacco pouch. In this, he is at the opposite end of the scale from . . .

. . . the *Weekend Cottager,* who finds it difficult to cram enough supplies for a short weekend into a large Volvo Estate. He also takes his wife, three children (one of whom is not related to him), a large dog and a large lawn-mower that has been mended in town, for it is the belief of many townsmen, based perhaps on watching farmers, that to enjoy the country you must employ large pieces of machinery, preferably noisy. (They forget that farmers do not enjoy the country.)

Also in this category are the *Moto-Cross Scrambler,* the *Radio-Controlled Model Plane Freak* and the *Soldier On Manoeuvres on Salisbury Plain,* who are all dedicated to the proposition that noise = ecstasy. By a strange mutation of genes, there is an opposite category dedicated to the art of total silence. High above the country sky floats the *Weekend Glider;* nearer the ground we can see the flashing and swooping, and occasionally crashing, of the *Hang Glider,* while on the ground itself we can see what was once a nearly extinct species, the *Balloonist.*

I have a cousin in Scotland who once found a balloonist in his fields, struggling to take off. Being a farmer, my cousin had gone out with a gun to shoot him, but he desisted at the last moment when he recognised the balloonist to be none other than *David Attenborough,* the only known example of this particular species. The David Attenborough has a unique migratory pattern, flying all over the world in search of good light and other very rare species like himself. The balloon, of course, was not his; after a week's hire it was due to be rented out for the making of a TV commercial and would be occupied by a *Fashion Model,* thus bringing us back to the start of our chain of human ecology.

It is useful to recognise all these species — in the case of my cousin and David Attenborough, absolutely vital — and it can give us all added pleasure if we feel we are sharing in the colourful pattern which keeps the countryside occupied, at least by day. Perhaps you can have fun spotting species which I haven't mentioned, and trying to fit them into the chain. For instance, there is the Lone Mountaineer, dangling helplessly from the cliff face by his multi-coloured ropes; the Teacher and His Group of Boys, probably with a Mountain Rescue Team close behind; the Orienteer, dressed only in his underwear, and so on.

Good luck!

Free Extra Section

Herbs and Spices

An optional extra section
for added flavour

As with all things in nature, there are far too many herbs and spices, and far too many books about them. I don't know about you, but every time I read a breathless account of how a simple infusion of dog's padwort can cure my shingles, clear my blood and stop my hair falling out, I feel worse not better.

So, as a final bouquet garni for this book, here is a rationalised list of all known herbs and spices, reduced to ten. Herbs and spices are not really part of nature, they are part of the publishing, packaging and prettification industry, but I feel convinced that this small extra section will add zest to your life and make you feel much healthier. It should be read every time you feel the urge to cook ground elder or wash your face in dandelion tea. The urge will soon go away.

ROUGHAGE

Any Frondwort that suddenly sprouts pink, yellow or purple flowers is a Roughage. This pretty old English herb is wonderful in Pimm's No 1, cakes and vases. It is said to cure quinsy, tansy, whimsy, comfrey and inglenook.

(Note: no herb ever cures anything, it is only *said* to cure something. This is always based on the testimony of somebody called Cuthbert who died in 1678. No one ever says what he died of. The odds are he took an overdose of Roughage but it was hushed up.)

CULPEPPER

Culpepper was the herb widely used in the Middle Ages as a cure for gout, dropsy, scurvy, infidelity, ague, mimsy and whickering. Round about 1700 it suddenly stopped curing all these things, for reasons we do not yet quite understand. In its natural form it is a tall, handsome green plant growing wild in ditches or tame in Tudor herb gardens. Nobody ever sees it growing like this, only in the form in which it is preferred by health food shops: a thin brown dust in an expensive sachet.

(Health food shops prefer everything in the form of a thin brown dust. As they stress the importance of naturalness as well, there seems to be a contradiction here.)

FOOL'S LEMON MINT

This is a rather attractive green plant with green leaves and green flowers which grows wild in other people's gardens. Take off a leaf, rub it between your fingers and smell it. It has absolutely no odour, but such is the power of the imagination that you will immediately detect a strong fragrance of lemon, verbena, Roger et Gallet, spearmint or whatever it is you wish to smell. Can be used in soups, stews, cakes and long hot baths with no harmful effects of any kind.

FRONDWORT

The basic English herb. It is an attractive green feathery plant and can be used in soups, stews, cakes and long hot baths. Of course, all other herbs look the same and can be used the same way, except Long Straight Dried Pod, but Frondwort is different because it actually tastes of something. Quite what is difficult to make out. Parsley? Grass cuttings? Liquorice all-sorts? Swimming pools? No matter — it is excellent in salads and on the covers of books about herbs.

ALLSPICE

A handy name given to anything not so far covered in this section. It is brown, shrivelled, aromatic and expensive. Also known as Crabtree and Evelyn, it makes an ideal gift.

CUMMIN OR GARDEN INDIAN HERB

This grows in boxes on the pavement outside Asian grocers' shops. It comes in long limp green fronds and is ideal for buying, taking home and showing off to friends, who don't know what it is, just like you. Take it back to the shop and swap it for the cooking version, which is known as . . .

YELLOW INDIAN DUST

Despite its name, this may be yellow, brown, blue, purple or cardboard-coloured. Beware versions which claim to be made in England, or to be 'the produce of various countries'; the only true version is that made by Mrs J. Veeraswama, 39 Calcutta Mansions, Old Bangapur, Utter Pradesh, India. It can be used in stews, soups, sauces, curries, long hot baths or anything you want to turn bright orange.

LONG STRAIGHT DRIED POD

This, as the name suggests, looks like a mummified stick insect. Perhaps that's what it is. It grows in the back of kitchen cupboards. It is excellent if dipped briefly into sweet sauces and puddings. It is not quite so excellent if dipped in cakes, as it makes them hard to fit into the oven. It is not so suitable for using in long hot baths, as it will either stab you or disappear down the plug-hole, though it is quite good for cleaning those awkward corners that feather dusters won't reach and as an emergency back-scratcher.

ALFALFARAFIA

A delightful little grass-like herb which is grown from tiny seeds which come from tiny packets found on revolving stands in garden centres. Sprinkle the seeds on a piece of old flannel, keep moist for six days in a darkened room, and you will have a fine crop of green seedlings tasting of old flannel — indeed, it is hard to tell where the flannel stops and the alfalfarafia starts. Ideal for use in long hot baths, if you have lost your old flannel.

127

DYNAMITE PEPPER

A tiny, dried curved fruit which can be yellow, red or any other colour, sometimes in powdered form. Can be added to anything to produce an effect of clutching your mouth, leaping around the room and yelling for water, though most Indian restaurants will administer copious draughts of lager as emergency first aid. Gangrene, scurvy, malaria, leprosy and cholera are just a few of the diseases it will not cure, but by God it takes your mind off them.